T0288395

CONCISE
LINCOLN
LIBRARY

—

EDITED BY RICHARD W. ETULAIN

AND SYLVIA FRANK RODRIGUE

MICHAEL S. GREEN

# Lincoln and
# Native Americans

Southern Illinois University Press
*Carbondale*

Southern Illinois University Press
www.siupress.com

24  23  22  21    4  3  2  1

The Concise Lincoln Library has been made possible in part
through a generous donation by the Leland E. and LaRita
R. Boren Trust.
    Volumes in this series have been published with support
from the Abraham Lincoln Bicentennial Foundation, dedicated to perpetuating and expanding Lincoln's vision for
America and completing America's unfinished work.

Jacket illustration adapted from a painting by Wendy Allen

Library of Congress Cataloging-in-Publication Data
Names: Green, Michael S., author.
Title: Lincoln and Native Americans / Michael S. Green.
Description: Carbondale : Southern Illinois University
Press, [2021] | Series: Concise Lincoln library | Includes
bibliographical references and index.
Identifiers: LCCN 2020042295 (print) |
LCCN 2020042296 (ebook) | ISBN 9780809338252 (cloth) |
ISBN 9780809338269 (ebook)
Subjects: LCSH: Lincoln, Abraham, 1809–1865—Relations
with Indians of North America. | Indians of North
America—Government relations. | United States—Politics
and government—1861–1865.
Classification: LCC E457.2.N6 G74 2021 (print) |
LCC E457.2.N6 (ebook) | DDC 973.7092—dc23
LC record available at https://lccn.loc.gov/2020042295
LC ebook record available at https://lccn.loc.gov/2020042296

*To Andy Fry and Alden Vaughan*

*For Robert Green and Eugene Moehring*

# CONTENTS

*Gallery of illustrations beginning on page 59*

LINCOLN AND NATIVE AMERICANS

# INTRODUCTION

A braham Lincoln ordered the largest mass execution and commutation in American history—for the same event, the Dakota
uprising of 1862. Lincoln could be compassionate and distant, as his
dealings with Native Americans show. He believed in reform, or
never could have been a Republican or antislavery, but doubted the
efficacy of reform movements that put morality above political action.
A masterful politician, moderate, and man of his time, he shared or
tolerated attitudes now viewed as troubling or even abhorrent but
was capable of growth and change. How quick he could be to effect
change depended on forces swirling around and within him.

That understanding of Lincoln guides what follows. The literature
on Lincoln and on Native Americans is rich indeed. To analyze all
sides of this equation would produce a far longer book. Some of the
writing on Lincoln and on Native Americans, and both, appears
in the text or notes. Although I intend this work to be accessible
and acceptable to those who study Lincoln and those who study
Native Americans, it belongs to a series on Lincoln, and Lincoln is
the focus here.

Scholars seeking to divine Lincoln's racial attitudes have varied
from claiming near perfection to calling him an ardent white su-
premacist, to the view captured in the title of George Fredrickson's
*Big Enough to Be Inconsistent.* But almost all have addressed slavery
and emancipation, with little attention to Native Americans—and
then mainly the Dakota or the Black Hawk War of 1832. The leading

biographies tend to deal briefly with Lincoln's best-known encounters with Native Americans, and Phillip Paludan's superb study of his presidency disposes of them in one long paragraph. "Lincoln may not have had any special animus toward Indians but he shared the widespread conviction that they lacked civilization and constituted an obstacle to the economic development of the West," Eric Foner has pointed out, and called Lincoln's policies "depressingly similar to those of virtually every nineteenth-century president."[1]

The only book-length monograph on this subject, David A. Nichols's excellent *Lincoln and the Indians*, delineates the Civil War years but says little about his prepresidential years. Other works have examined key events and Native peoples of Lincoln's presidency, or the role of Native American soldiers in the war. This study unifies these threads by considering his actions and attitudes in light of his earlier years and of family encounters that predated his birth.[2]

To understate the case, the literature on these subjects is enormous. Among the ways scholars have examined Native Americans in the nineteenth century, a few help explain Lincoln, his era, or both. One is that most Anglos saw them as a separate or at least distinct race, whereas today many Indigenous people consider themselves citizens of independent nations within the United States and object to being considered a minority race (this links to the issue of race as a social construct; as Nell Irvin Painter put it, "race is an idea, not a fact"). Some scholars have called for studying them in connection with foreign relations, because they belonged to independent nations, and driving them from their ancestral lands was imperialistic and expansionist. Granting the point, Lincoln referred matters involving them to the Interior Department, not the State Department; within the government, the agencies involved with Natives will be the focus here.[3]

A related point involves settler colonialism. As Patrick Wolfe's "Settler Colonialism and the Elimination of the Native" argues, "Settler colonialism destroys to replace." Referring to the Trail of Tears, the most famous (but not only) American example, Wolfe wrote, "Why should genteel Georgians wish to rid themselves of such cultivated neighbours? The reason why the Cherokee's constitution and their agricultural prowess stood out as such singular provocations to the officials and legislators of the state of Georgia . . . is that the Cherokee's farms, plantations, slaves and written constitution all signified *permanence*." Andrew Jackson and his allies wanted their land. As Walter Hixson has noted, "Settler colonialism typically unfolds in association with nation building"—in which Lincoln and his predecessors and contemporaries engaged. The ensuing violence led to terms like genocide or ethnic cleansing, and deterritorialization and reterritorialization to explain how colonial powers cleared the land of native species and people, especially in the Third World. Europeans' imperialism did much to shape North America and eliminated as much of the Native presence as possible as they were "superimposing their own values and institutions upon it."[4]

Lincoln's role in and view of settler colonialism and deterritorializing in the United States will unfold here, though these interpretations mainly loom in the background. To league Lincoln with Jackson, for example, goes too far on the basis of the evidence. Clearly, many Americans sought to dispossess Native Americans of their land and culture. Lincoln might be called a participant who was unthinking except when he took time to think about it. Then, he voiced displeasure with the situation that Indigenous people faced but did little about it because of the war for the Union and emancipation, which mattered more to him and most others; the difficulties in changing a system that profited politicians and businesspeople whose support he sought and needed; his prejudices and inclinations; the capital and population expansion that conflicted with the Natives' presence; and his political sense, which made it evident that many Americans had no intention of treating Indians equally or fairly. Obviously, it cannot be known what he might have done if he had lived.

This contribution to the Concise Lincoln Library examines these issues, what Lincoln said and did with regard to Native Americans, and the events and ideas that influenced him or that he had to contemplate. As much as possible, the focus will be on Lincoln. I have benefited enormously from scholars of Native American history but make no pretensions to being an ethnohistorian, nor will I constantly address what happens in the context of the interpretations mentioned above.

One problem should be addressed at the outset: while Lincoln is the focus, he disappears at times in the ensuing pages, even during his presidency. To explain what went on requires discussions of events far from him and of people who represented him but never communicated with him. The situation was comparable in some ways to royal officials in the Thirteen Colonies, and representatives of the United States and other nations in foreign lands before instant communication was possible. They acted as they thought their superiors wanted or as they considered best for their government. For example, Lincoln did not authorize the Sand Creek Massacre, but his appointees were crucial to it.[5]

In addition, this is unabashedly a history of Lincoln and Native Americans. Where applicable, I explain what ensued after Lincoln, or where his policies led. But for the most part, this story ends at 7:22 a.m. on April 15, 1865. Not because nothing of importance happened afterward, but to keep the focus where it belongs: as the title suggests, on Lincoln and Native Americans.

Six chapters and a conclusion follow. Chapter 1 examines Lincoln's ancestry and early years to help clarify the views he developed on Native Americans. Chapter 2 delves into his prepresidential career in relation to Native peoples, including his service in the Black Hawk War, the Whig Party, his marriage, and the Republican Party. Chapter 3 focuses on the people around him who were making policy and dealing with Native Americans, the reformers who tried to change them, and how Lincoln's main personal encounter with Native Americans as president showed the difficulty those reformers faced.

The next three chapters deal with important issues involving Native Americans during Lincoln's presidency. Chapter 4 addresses Indian Territory and how Lincoln erred at the start, then ran into political problems in trying to correct the error. Chapter 5 describes the Dakota uprising in 1862, why it happened, and how Lincoln and his administration responded. Chapter 6 takes a geographic approach to how Lincoln and Republicans faced westward and discusses the contradictions involved in their free labor ideology and in opening the Far West to homesteaders and railroad builders. It looks at the regions of the West and at similarities and differences in policy. The conclusion assesses Lincoln's words and deeds in relation to Native Americans and what they mean.

Both primary and secondary accounts drive this work. I am deeply indebted to Nichols's *Lincoln and the Indians* and to students of Lincoln and his time and place. I have changed some inconsistent capitalization in nineteenth-century writing, especially by William Herndon as he wrote out interviews with Lincoln's family and friends, but otherwise avoid corrections. I try to use proper terminology in referring to Native American groups—the Dakota, for example, instead of the Sioux, except when quoting others. I interchangeably use *Indigenous people, Native Americans, Native people, Indians,* and similar terms. I intend no disrespect, inaccuracy, or opacity, but this reflects the varied terms used by Native peoples—their diversity and that of the Anglos who fought them, sometimes tried and more often refused to accept or understand them, and sought to help them as they considered best. To cite one such person: Abraham Lincoln.

## BEGINNINGS

A braham Lincoln's ancestors lived at the center and on the periphery of the links between English, African, and Native American. English settlers arrived in the New World with an image of Native people that changed. They distinguished between civilized (themselves) and uncivilized and savage (Natives). With persuasion and force that varied by their faith and location, colonists tried to convert Native peoples to Christianity and English ways. They failed.

That failure and attitudes about skin color shaped how Americans viewed Indigenous people. As historian Alden Vaughan pointed out in a study of these perceptions, English settlers originally saw them as almost equally light-skinned and thus capable of being "assimilated into colonial society as soon as they succumbed to English social norms and Protestant theology." But "a confluence of European and American ideas and events" prompted Americans to view them instead as inferior, reducing them from nurture to nature: Natives, they believed, lacked the ability to be part of American culture and society. The world in which Lincoln grew up, and from which he descended, could not conceive of Indigenous people as equal members of society.[1]

Neither Lincoln's racial attitudes nor those of American society proved static. Amid few believers in racial equality, he suffered from some common biases of the time. His political idol, Henry Clay, privately called Indians "essentially inferior" and "not an improvable breed," but publicly declared that mistreating them would "subject us, as a nation, to the reproaches of all good men, and . . . bring down upon us the maledictions of a more exalted and powerful tribunal." Lincoln's contradictions reflected his times and origins.[2]

## "Not in Battle, but by Stealth"

The events that formed Lincoln's views of Native Americans predated his birth. "My paternal grandfather, Abraham Lincoln, emigrated from Rockingham County, Virginia, to Kentucky, about 1781 or 2, where, a year or two later, he was killed by Indians, not in battle, but by stealth, when he was laboring to open a farm in the forest," he wrote in a short autobiography. His summary was largely accurate. What happened to his family could have made him a violent enemy of all things Indian. While it did not, it shaped his early life and image of himself and fit into a long family history.[3]

Lincoln was curious about that history. He said, "I believe the first of our ancestors we know anything about was Samuel Lincoln, who came from Norwich, England, in 1638, and settled in a small Massachusetts place called Hingham, or it might have been Hanghim." Drollery aside, Lincoln was mostly right. Sources suggest Samuel Lincoln arrived in 1637, a year before his most famous descendant thought. Like many migrants, Samuel followed a family member, his older brother Thomas. They came from the English region for which Massachusetts settlers named the towns of Hingham and Norwich.[4]

Unlike the Puritans before and after them, the first Lincolns apparently neither encountered nor created major problems with Indigenous people. When Samuel settled about fifteen miles southeast of Boston, the nearby Native populace had suffered a devastating smallpox epidemic. The colony was fighting Indians about a hundred miles southwest of Hingham in the Pequot War of 1637, which followed disputes over the fur trade involving the English and Dutch, climate issues that reduced the availability of food, and intertribal conflicts. Samuel Lincoln and other settlers reaped the benefits of driving Native Americans from their land. The Massachusetts, the tribe nearest Hingham, tended not to be warlike; if anything they supported the Puritans when they fought other Indians.[5]

A century after the first Lincolns arrived, the family joined an internal migration. They went west and south, to New Jersey and then southeastern Pennsylvania. There, in Berks County, Abraham Lincoln's great-great-grandfather Mordecai lived in Amity, reportedly named for the relations between Native residents and Swedish settlers. But the town could have been misnamed: Mordecai also was a commissioner tasked with defending the community against Indians.[6]

After the French and Indian War (1754–63) and the Paxton Boys' uprising against Native Americans, the Lincolns pushed west from Pennsylvania. In 1766 John Lincoln, his son Abraham, and their family moved to Virginia's Shenandoah Valley and a six-hundred-acre farm near Linville Creek. In 1774, as one of Lord Dunmore's army in western Virginia, Abraham fought the Shawnee, whose defeat opened the area to more white settlers. As a Revolutionary militiaman, he served under General Lachlan McIntosh in an unsuccessful fight against Indians at Fort Detroit.[7]

In late 1779, like his ancestors, Captain Abraham Lincoln went farther west. Although the Revolutionary War continued, and no government officials or military could ease the threats posed by Natives upset with intrusions on their land, the Lincolns traveled 250 miles over the Cumberland Gap with Daniel Boone, a cousin through marriage who had carved out the trail. Virginians like the Lincolns comprised a large number of the approximately two hundred thousand migrants to Kentucky, their "new found Paradise." A relative recalled that the move included "several fights with the Indians during their journey by which they lost several of their party." Some of the fights may have been with the Shawnee whom Captain Lincoln battled during the Revolution; he allegedly had to "run the gauntlet" after being captured and then they let him go. Continuing their journey, the Lincolns settled on about five thousand acres.[8]

What happened there shaped the future president's life. As Lincoln's cousin Dennis Hanks put it, "In Kentucky all men had to clear out their own field," including splitting trees into rails for fences. Early in 1786, Captain Lincoln was working on a fence with his youngest son Thomas, then about eight years old, nearby, and older sons Mordecai and Josiah in an adjacent field. A group of Shawnee attacked the farm. One shot and killed Abraham. Josiah ran for help at the nearest fort, two miles away. Mordecai headed to the house, grabbed his rifle, and climbed to the loft. He saw an Indian had picked up Thomas by the neck and seat of his pants and started to run off with him. Another Indian tried to warn Thomas's captor about the porthole with a rifle peeking out. Mordecai aimed at a silver pendant in the shape of a half-moon dangling from the Indian's neck and fired. The shot hit him. Thomas ran for the house; his mother opened the door and let him in. By the time Josiah returned with help, the fight had ended.[9]

Although Mordecai Lincoln called the silver pendant "the prettiest mark he held a rifle on," seeing his father die in an ambush left him virulently anti-Indian. One relative recounted that Mordecai "swore eternal vengeance on all Indian[s,] an oath which he faithfully kept as he afterward during times of profound peace with the Indians killed several of them," and let others know he had done so. When he lived in Grayson County, Kentucky, one acquaintance reported, he heard reports of Native Americans nearby. Mordecai grabbed his rifle, jumped on his horse, and disappeared for two days. "When he returned he said he left one Lying in a sink hole for the Indians had killed his farther [sic] and he was determined to have satisfaction."[10]

Thomas Lincoln turned out differently. Thomas's son said, "Uncle Mord had run off with all the talents of the family." As the oldest son, through primogeniture, Mordecai obtained most of Captain Abraham's land and apparently sent Thomas out of the family home at age twelve. Abraham Lincoln may have admired his uncle for saving Thomas, but his grandfather's death set in motion events that affected his regard for his father. Left to fend for himself, Thomas became "a wandering, laboring boy," then a farmer. In his teens he spent a month in the Kentucky militia, but whether he saw Native peoples or had any opinion of them remains unknown; he regaled others with accounts of his service and exploits involving Daniel Boone, so he may have discussed them. Thomas's step-grandson Thomas L. D. Johnston called Lincoln's father "a humorous man: he was a social man—loved Company. . . . He read his bible—told Indian stories—that thrilled my young nature." One of the stories he told Johnston and others described the circumstances of his father's death well enough for several to repeat the tale to William Herndon when he conducted interviews about the grandson named for Captain Abraham Lincoln.[11]

Especially where few sources exist, historians long have debated Lincoln's policies and actions, and his relations with family members. His father's near kidnapping is an enigmatic example. According to Hanks, who lived with the Lincolns in Indiana and Illinois, "the Indian dropt Thomas—ran and was followed by the blood the next day & found dead—in his flight he threw his gun in a tree top which was found." Augustus Chapman, Hanks's son-in-law, recounted that when Mordecai fired, "the Indian bounded high into the air and fell dead." Granting that their memories may have varied, this minor difference could mean that Thomas changed or embellished details—a common issue in understanding his son's life.[12]

Embellished or not, the background of Lincoln's mother is murkier. Nancy Hanks may have been Lucy Hanks's illegitimate daughter, but her family tree reveals roots, and linkages to Native peoples, as complex as the Lincoln side. Some studies show the first Hanks family members in the New World reaching Plymouth, Massachusetts, during the 1690s. More recent research suggests her first American ancestor, Thomas, arrived in Virginia early in the 1650s from Malmesbury, England, about 225 miles southwest of Norwich, from which Samuel Lincoln migrated. Hanks settled in Virginia's "northern neck," near the center of the Powhatan Confederacy—the group of Indigenous people led by Powhatan and then his brother Opechancanough, who twice attacked and nearly destroyed Jamestown. By the time Thomas Hanks reached Chesapeake Bay in the 1650s, the Confederacy generally sided with the English against other Native groups and was in decline.[13]

Like the Lincolns, the Hanks family headed west. Joseph Hanks, born in the northern neck of the bay in 1725, moved to present-day West Virginia, where his granddaughter Nancy was born in 1784. Then Joseph and his wife, children, and granddaughter Nancy went through the Cumberland Gap and settled about fifty miles south of the Lincolns. A decade later, near where the Hanks family lived in the Rolling Fork area, settlers and Indians fought their supposed "last battle . . . in this part of Kentucky."[14]

Like Thomas Lincoln, Nancy Hanks had a story. When she lived with her uncle Richard Berry's family, another girl resided there: Sarah Mitchell, her orphaned first cousin, who lost her mother when migrants and Indians fought at Defeated Camp near modern-day London, Kentucky. When her family and others apparently celebrated their good luck in avoiding Indian problems as they crossed the Appalachians, they failed to post a guard. Sarah was one of the few who survived the ensuing attacks. According to family stories, the Indians took Sarah to Canada, and her father died pursuing them across the Ohio River. Her grandmother wrote to various officials seeking her "redemption from captivity." She returned after less than five years following the Treaty of Greenville, which ended significant fighting between Natives and white people in present-day Ohio in 1795. Sarah then joined the Berry family and eleven-year-old Nancy Hanks. When Nancy married Thomas Lincoln, they named their first child for Sarah, who had a daughter named Nancy.[15]

In 1809 the Lincolns welcomed another child, Abraham. How much they encountered Indians near Sinking Springs Farm is unknown. When Abraham Lincoln was two years old, a Shawnee apparently killed a man who moved onto land the Indian frequented along nearby Little Pigeon Creek. Other settlers killed the Shawnee and his leader, a subchief named Setteedown, whose ghost supposedly haunted the settlement.[16]

These events shaped Lincoln in distinct ways. His family's past could have prompted deep feelings about Native Americans. If his father shared Mordecai's attitudes and his mother related her cousin's saga, Lincoln might have inherited his uncle's hatred; no evidence suggests he did. But that attack affected Thomas Lincoln's future and his son's. Had his father survived, Thomas might have led a more prosperous life that might not have included Nancy Hanks. Although a child between eight and ten at the time of his family's deadly encounter with Native Americans, Thomas remembered it clearly enough to regale two generations with the story. His son developed storytelling talents, too.[17]

## Lincoln, Native Americans, and Books

In the 1820s an Indiana teenager with little access to schooling obtained *History of the United States from Their Earliest Settlement as Colonies to the Cession of Florida in Eighteen Hundred and Twenty-One*. William Grimshaw's text celebrated much, but not what he saw as twin evils. One, slavery, he blamed on greed. The other was that colonizers had no "just claim upon the property of the native possessors," but took it anyway. Grimshaw saw Indians as savages defeated in the march of progress by superior people, but still as humans who were wronged. Analyzing Lincoln as a writer, Fred Kaplan refers to Grimshaw's work as describing "a nation with a destiny that required applying Enlightenment values and humanitarian principles to the national condition. American history was and would be a steady march forward." If Grimshaw influenced Lincoln's views on politics and slavery, he may have affected how he felt about Native people.[18]

What other books could have led him to similar conclusions? "Abe read no books in Kentucky," Dennis Hanks said. In Indiana, Lincoln read Aesop's *Fables*, *Pilgrim's Progress*, and the Bible but emerged skeptical about religion. He read *Robinson Crusoe*, in which Friday was an Indigenous person who accepted cannibalism but proved loyal to Crusoe and capable of conversion to Christianity. He may have encountered *The Autobiography of Benjamin Franklin*, which referred to savages but included Franklin warning a British officer against the tactics of "Indians, who, by constant practice, are dexterous in laying and executing them," only to be dismissed for thinking the British incapable of dealing with them, and being proved right.[19]

Lincoln read two of the most popular books on George Washington. In Parson Mason Weems's *Life of Washington*, he encountered "the low sensuality of the Indian, ready, for a *dram*, to lift the tomahawk," and Washington's refusal to avenge their wrongdoing. In *The Life of George Washington*, David Ramsay called them "numerous, accustomed to war, and not without discipline," and praised those who, "from their vicinity and intercourse with the white people, had attained a degree of civilization, exceeding what was usual amongst savages." He lauded Washington for "judicious treatment" in the French and Indian War, when "friendly Indians" helped him. Ramsay credited Washington's presidency with bringing peace with Indians, and "the prospect of meliorating the condition of the savages, is daily brightening; for the system first begun by Washington, with a view of civilizing these fierce sons of nature, has been ever since steadily pursued, by all his successors." In the 1832 edition, which Lincoln may not have read, editor Grimshaw added, "Except general Jackson; by whom, a different policy has been pursued, in relation to the Creeks and Cherokees."[20]

Other texts may have affected Lincoln. Alexander Lowe's *Columbian Class Book* included interactions in which Native people could be violent but often proved thoughtful. In Caleb Bingham's *The American Preceptor*, he may have read about "The Humane Indian," an account of a planter denying help to an Indian, then receiving aid from the same Indian. Bingham concluded, "It is not difficult to say which of these two men had the best claim to the name of Christian." Thomas Lincoln apparently provided his son with a collection of speeches that included brief declarations from Native leaders about their unjust treatment.[21]

How this reading affected Lincoln's views, especially about Native Americans, is uncertain. But he left evidence of why it may have mattered. He told his friend Joshua Speed, "I am slow to learn and slow to forget that which I have learned. My mind is like a piece of steel, very hard to scratch any thing on it and almost impossible after you get it there to rub it out." Later, when his law partner Herndon was annoyed at his habit of reading aloud, he said, "When I read aloud my two senses catch the idea—first I see what I am reading and secondly I hear it read; and I can thus remember what I read the better." Because Lincoln remembered what he read and in his youth reread the few books to which he had access, what he learned clearly stuck. Herndon's cousin later said Lincoln "had the Best memory of any man I Ever Knew" and "Never forgot any thing he Read."[22]

When the Lincolns moved to Indiana, where young Abraham did this reading, recent history suggested they might see Native Americans.

In 1816 the Lincolns reached present-day Spencer County, on land the Indigenous populace ceded in treaties negotiated by former territorial governor William Henry Harrison, for whom Lincoln later campaigned for president. The main cession, in August 1804, involved the Delaware and the Piankashaw, both connected with the Miami nation. After arriving in southwestern Indiana, the family lived close to the Lenape or Delaware tribe that once dwelled in New Jersey and Pennsylvania, near earlier generations of Lincolns. Dennis Hanks, who came with the Lincolns, said, "No Indians there when I first went to Indiana." Their absence appealed to Thomas Lincoln and others hoping to escape land-title disputes in the Bluegrass State; so many moved that, one observer claimed, "Kentucky had taken Indiana without firing a shot."[23]

Treaties changed who controlled the land, but peace was another matter. The Lincolns lived about two hundred miles south of where Harrison became known as "Ol' Tippecanoe" by defeating Tecumseh and his brother Tenskwatawa, "the Prophet," who hoped to stop white encroachment. Native resistance in Indiana significantly declined, although they still battled settlers. During the War of 1812, Indians, encouraged by the British in Canada, attacked Pigeon Roost in present-day Scott County, about eighty miles from where the Lincolns later settled. They also burned a building about 120 miles north of Spencer County at Fort Harrison, named for the territorial governor and defended by Captain Zachary Taylor, another figure in Lincoln's life.[24]

No evidence suggests Lincoln knew about these events. The only reference to Native Americans in his hand in Indiana appears in his childhood "copybook." After a verse—"Abraham Lincoln / his hand and pen / he will be good but / god knows When"—he refers to days "swift as an indian arr[ow]," suggesting awareness of them and possibly their impact on him. A schoolmate recalled him choosing a topic to discuss, "Who has the most right to complain, the Indian or the Negro?" and talking about it while working in the fields. Whatever he argued, African Americans received most of his attention in the future—but in the near future, Native Americans had a greater impact on his life and career.[25]

## To Illinois

In 1831 Lincoln accompanied his family to Illinois. Several Hanks family members moved or wanted to relocate to Macon County; with two of them married to daughters of his stepmother Sarah Bush Johnston Lincoln, the rest followed. They settled west of Decatur along the Sangamon River, about two hundred miles northwest of their Indiana home, for three years before moving east to Coles County.[26]

The Native American presence in central Illinois had declined by the time the Lincolns arrived. Congress created Illinois Territory nine days before Lincoln's birth in 1809, after many years of government officials and investors buying or taking Native lands. In several treaties, the tribes comprising the Illinois Confederation and known as the Illini, and the Sauk and Fox or Mesquakie, conceded much of their land. The group most prominent along the Sangamon, the Kickapoo, had largely been forced to leave. During the War of 1812, an Illinois pioneer, Ninian Edwards, burned one of their villages; his son married Elizabeth Todd, who had a younger sister named Mary. Lincoln met the Edwards and Todd families in Springfield, but first he moved down the Sangamon to New Salem and encountered Native Americans in different ways than he did through family stories or books.[27]

# MILITIAS AND MOSQUITOES

### The Black Hawk War

A year after moving to New Salem, Lincoln served in one of the many Indian wars of his time. As with so many other such conflicts, the Black Hawk War reflected Americans' mistreatment and misperceptions of Indians, and desire for their land. After the War of 1812, the Sauk and Mesquakie agreed to a federal treaty to sell their land, then move west, out of Illinois. In the late 1820s, during the Indians' winter hunt, squatters occupied their land, built fences, cleared out their homes, and attacked Native peoples who tried to stop them. When the Sauk and Mesquakie avenged an earlier raid by killing twenty-five Menominee, President Andrew Jackson, Secretary of War Lewis Cass, and Governor John Reynolds of Illinois seized their opportunity for reasons related to politics, policy, or both. They sent soldiers after the "murderers" and encouraged other Native peoples to attack Black Hawk's Sauk tribe.[1]

The related battles became known as the Black Hawk War of 1832. Black Hawk had no desire to fight—"My object was not *war!*" he said—but saw no alternative. He had various reasons to return to Illinois in 1832: he believed in his people's right to the land, wanted to avoid an attack by another tribe, and was angry at longtime rival Keokuk, who gained influence by working with white settlers instead of resisting them. Reports spread that villagers disinterred Native peoples from burial sites, and the food supply the federal government promised began to run out. More than two thousand Sauk, Mesquakie, and Winnebago backed Black Hawk, but many Natives tried to stay neutral, or opposed Black Hawk in hopes of improving their relations with the federal and state governments. For their part, Americans feared an Indian confederation and British interference in Native affairs. Ultimately, one-third of the army and about ten thousand Illinois militiamen fought for fewer than five months. Seventy-two white people and six hundred to a thousand Natives died.[2]

Black Hawk faced long odds. Cass called out the army and Reynolds the Illinois militia, meaning white males of ages eighteen to forty-five. Winning the first major battle, at Stillman's Run on May 14, 1832, Black Hawk expressed surprise at how badly the Illinoisans fought but saw how badly outnumbered he was. With Jackson egging them on from Washington, federal and state troops drove Black Hawk into Wisconsin. On August 2 at Bad Axe, as Black Hawk put it, some of his followers hoping to escape by crossing the Mississippi "tried to give themselves up—the whites paid no attention to their entreaties—but commenced *slaughtering* them!" About 150 of Black Hawk's group survived.[3]

New treaties took more Native land, and in a harbinger of the next major removal, relocating Black Hawk's band to modern-day Iowa and Kansas cost more lives than the war did. Black Hawk went east before traveling to his new home and won admiration for his dignity and decency. That may have affected Lincoln's description of his own role in the war less than his instincts for politics and humor. But he managed to capitalize on his military experience, denigrate it, and take pride in it.[4]

Lincoln may have minimized his service because it was minimal. He entered the militia on April 28, 1832, joined the Fourth Regiment of Mounted Volunteers in Samuel Whiteside's brigade, and marched to Rock Island to be sworn into federal service on May 9. The militia went to Dixon's Ferry and Ottawa and disbanded on May 27 without fighting. Lincoln then reenlisted for twenty days as a private in Captain Elijah Iles's mountain company (Second Lieutenant Robert Anderson, who later surrendered Fort Sumter under

President Lincoln, signed him up). Iles's troops, a "spy battalion" used for scouting, marched to Galena amid reports that Indians had cut off the town. Lincoln then enrolled for thirty days with Jacob Early's company, mustering out at White River, Wisconsin, on July 10. With their horses stolen, he and messmate George Harrison went 450 miles to Peoria, walking and riding horses belonging to other militiamen. Then Lincoln and Harrison bought a canoe, headed down the Illinois River to Havana, and walked to New Salem.[5]

The facts seem simple, but Lincoln's seventy-three days of service meant much to him then and later. When the war began, he needed a job. After moving to Illinois in 1831, he left home for New Salem. He clerked at Denton Offutt's store, which was about to "wink out" as Lincoln put it. He later told law partner William Herndon, whose cousins lived in New Salem, that "I was out of work, and there being no danger of more fighting, I could do nothing better than enlist again." Lincoln later received about $125 from the army for serving two and a half months. Unfortunately, he opened a store with William Berry, and it went under, creating what Lincoln called the "national debt." The Black Hawk War proved less of a financial boon than it might have.[6]

Nor did the war expose him to actual combat. According to Herndon, Lincoln recalled burying men killed and scalped at Kellogg's Grove in northern Illinois while serving under Early. He remembered that "the red light of the morning sun was streaming upon them as they lay heads towards us on the ground. And every man had a round, red spot on top of his head, about as big as a dollar where the redskins had taken his scalp. It was frightful, but it was grotesque, and the red sunlight seemed to paint everything all over. I remember that one man had on buckskin breeches." Royal Clary, one of his company, saw mutilated women and children, and "strong men wept at this—hard hearted men Cried." Harrison claimed that after a battle near Galena, Lincoln and two other men searched the woods for a wounded young chief and discovered his body. Lincoln and the others encouraged General Alexander Posey to pursue nearby Indians, to no avail. After returning to New Salem, Lincoln and Harrison "saw a battle in full operation," but Lincoln said, "George, this can't be a very dangerous battle" because no one fell. They figured out it was a cavalry training exercise and went on their way. Lincoln, one acquaintance said, "expressed a desire to get into an engagement" so his men could "meet Powder & Lead," but never did.[7]

The Black Hawk War affected Lincoln in other ways. In New Salem, he impressed the Clary's Grove Boys, a roistering group of young men in the area, when he wrestled their leader. After joining the militia, which elected its officers, they backed him for captain against William Kirkpatrick. Lincoln won; even after legislative and congressional elections, he called that victory "a success which gave me more pleasure than any I have had since." Indeed, his friend William Greene recalled him saying, "I'll be damned, Bill, but I've beat him!"—the only time he heard Lincoln swear. Lincoln's friends claimed Kirkpatrick once hired and cheated Lincoln, then left the militia over his loss. But he stayed in the militia and when William Dean Howells told the story in drafting a campaign biography, Lincoln deleted the passage. He noted, "Wm. Kirkpatrick, I never worked for him."[8]

His service also taught Lincoln about leadership. One soldier called his unit "the hardest set of men he ever saw"; in response to his first order, they reportedly told him to "go to the devil." But he won them over, partly because Clary's Grove Boys leader Jack Armstrong was first sergeant, and through wrestling matches and entertaining his men with stories. But rather than fighting, the company "made war on the pigs and chickens" they stole. Lincoln paid for mischief: his superiors took his sword for a day after he fired his gun within fifty yards of camp and ordered him to carry a wooden sword for two days when his men broke into officers' quarters, filched their alcohol, and became too drunk to march, although one of his company called him "entirely blameless." According to one account, Lincoln led his men across a field but could not recall the command to get them through a gate. He said, "Halt! This company will break ranks for two minutes and form again on the other side of that gate!" Perhaps learning to improvise proved beneficial.[9]

He also avoided the "Indian hating" that one scholar called "part of the very character of society in the West." An older Native American entered Lincoln's camp with a letter from Cass vouching for him. His men said, "We have come out to fight the Indians and by God we intend to do so." He replied, "Men, this must not be done." When they called him "cowardly," Lincoln, "swarthy with resolution and rage," said, "If any man thinks I am a coward let him test it." Reminded that he was larger than any of them, he replied, "Choose your weapons." His threat, and the Clary's Grove Boys' support, eased the tension. When Howells included the story in his draft, Lincoln left it unchanged.[10]

The Black Hawk War also fostered friendships. Two militiamen described Lincoln as "the favorite of all of them and he loved all of them as they loved him," and as "idolized by his men and generally by all the Regiment & Core to which he belonged." Another said, "Very few men in the army could successfully compete with Mr Lincoln, either in wrestling or swimming; he well understood both arts. But his good humor & Quaint sayings, always preserved pleasant feeling." After mustering out, when he and Harrison walked with their company, Harrison said, "I laughed at our fate, and he joked at it, and we all started off merrily. The generous men of our Company walked and rode by turns with us, and we fared about equal with the rest."[11]

Lincoln took political advantage of his service. A militiaman said, "He was acquainted with nearly every body, and he had determined as he told me, to become a candidate for the next legislature," and rounded up support. A New Salem resident said, "I heard him making his first speech after returning from the Black Hawk war. He brushed up his hair from his tall dark forehead and said: 'Gentlemen I have just returned from the Campaign My Personal appearance is rather shabby & dark. I am almost as red as those men I have been chasing through the prairies & forests on the Rivers of Illinois.'" But, unable to campaign while in the militia, he lost the race. Lincoln later joked about his military tenure but "was rather proud of it after all," Herndon sensed.[12]

Lincoln reaped other benefits from the Black Hawk War—and not just because, two decades later, a congressional appropriation to veterans gave him 160 acres of land in Iowa. It helped him build a network with aspiring politicians like future congressmen Edward Baker and John J. Hardin, longtime ally Orville Browning, and John

Todd Stuart, who helped him win his next race in 1834 and then become a lawyer. Several scholars have cited his service as critical to his future leadership. Although Civil War soldiers knew little of his experiences, they felt he understood their lives. As Lincoln expert Frank Williams wrote, "Enthusiastic young volunteers could not make the transition from civilian to military life overnight, and there would never be a complete transition. Lincoln also understood that the troops' enthusiasm sometimes had little to do with patriotism and more to do with an independent streak in each of them." Further, his desire to pursue the Indians foreshadowed the Civil War, when he implored generals to follow the rebel army, often to no avail.[13]

Whether the Black Hawk War shaped his attitudes was another matter. "Although the incident with the old man is illustrative of Lincoln's humanity when confronted personally with Indians and Indian problems, his public attitude characteristically returned to one of detachment and political preoccupation," David Nichols wrote in his study of Lincoln and Native Americans. But when Lincoln could have been anti-Indian, in his treatment of the aged visitor during the war and in future political speeches, he declined opportunities that could have aided him politically. Perhaps the benefits of pay and connections were enough; perhaps, just as he claimed not to hate Confederates or his political foes, the same was true for Native Americans.[14]

### Whigs, a "Beau Ideal," and Indians

The prepresidential Abraham Lincoln called himself "always a Whig in politics." Actually, his first electoral foray—his legislative campaign in 1832—predated that party. Shortly thereafter, the Whigs evolved from remnants of the Federalists, with their probusiness views and belief in an assertive federal government; National Republicans who preferred a stronger central government than the more rigid Jeffersonians in the Democratic Party; and Anti-Masons who attacked secret societies and espoused what became Whig policies. Whigs "envisioned qualitative, not just quantitative, progress," historian Daniel Walker Howe noted in distinguishing them from Democrats. "Within an economically developed and integrated nation, Lincoln believed, individual autonomy could flourish as never before."[15]

The Whig Party survived for two decades but never quite prospered. Twice it ruptured after electing a president: William Henry Harrison won in 1840 and died after a month in office, and Vice-President John Tyler's Democratic loyalties left Whigs sidelined and fuming; Zachary Taylor won in 1848, and after he died in July 1850, his successor, Millard Fillmore, signed the Compromise of 1850, which Taylor and many antislavery northern Whigs opposed. The party did better at the state level but faced a conundrum. The Democratic ideology of individual liberty for white people, states' rights, and encouraging entrepreneurship served it everywhere, but the Whig belief in promoting internal improvements through federal activism troubled its southern branch. Not only would these advances empower the North, but if Whigs involved themselves in state economic issues, slavery could become a target. Southerners found that intolerable, and when slavery became the defining political issue in the 1850s, the Whig Party collapsed.[16]

Henry Clay led and epitomized the party, and Lincoln called him "my beau ideal of a statesman." A friend said, "Clay was his favorite of all the great men of the nation. He all but worshiped his name." They shared an attachment to the Union, a desire to reduce slavery, and a commitment to the "American System" of internal improvements. Democrats claimed to back state-funded improvements and fought the American System in part because it might promote federal interference with slavery. Lincoln welcomed state action: in the spirit of the New York governor behind the Erie Canal, he dreamed of being known as "the DeWitt Clinton of Illinois"; as a legislator, he pushed to build roads and canals, and for banking reform. Long before signing the Pacific Railroad Act, Lincoln declared that "at no distant day, a railroad, connecting the Eastern cities with some point on the Mississippi, will surely be built."[17]

But the growth of slavery, industry, or both long had been justifications to remove or assimilate Native Americans. George Washington's administration began the trend of negotiating with Natives to obtain land and merge them into the Anglo population. Nor was assimilation the only issue. Businessmen, settlers, and politicians at all levels of government competed to profit from land and trade. As

James Monroe's secretary of war, John Calhoun tried to assure respect for treaties but found that goal hard to achieve. Jackson derided "the farce of treating with Indian tribes" and Calhoun understood that Jackson spoke for the West, a region important to his own political ambitions.[18]

Jackson became the central contemporary and historical figure in Indian removal. His ally Martin Van Buren knew of "no measure, in the whole course of his administration, of which he was more exclusively the author than this." When Jackson planned to veto the Maysville Road Bill of 1830 and thereby block federal construction of a road within Clay's Kentucky, he held off until Congress had passed his Indian removal bill. Jackson wanted Native Americans off their land so that white settlers could have it, but he also saw them as a threat to American growth.[19]

When the desires of Jackson and his supporters motivated these policies toward Indians, Clay stirred to action. One of his supporters, George Prentice, wrote his biography and edited the *Louisville Journal*; Lincoln devoured both. Prentice's book included excerpts from Clay's speeches, which empathized with "pitiable" and "miserable" Indians suffering from Jackson's "barbarity," although Clay derided "Indian ignorance" in comparison with "our enlightened condition." New Salem friend Mentor Graham recalled Lincoln's "text book" as the *Louisville Journal*, which Prentice edited as Clay's organ. Lincoln could easily find out what his idol thought of Native peoples and of Jackson's treatment of them.[20]

Clay's position on Native peoples reflected ideology and politics. In a Cabinet meeting while serving as John Quincy Adams's secretary of state, Clay called it "impossible to civilize Indians. . . . They were destined to extinction, and, although he would never use or countenance inhumanity towards them, he did not think them, as a race, worth preserving." But as Jackson pursued their land and defied the Supreme Court, Clay urged assimilation: "Let us confer upon them, if we can, the inestimable blessings of Christianity, and civilization, and then, if they must sink beneath the progressive wave of civilized population, we are free from all reproach, and stand acquitted in the sight of God and man." Clay objected less to Indian removal than to how it was done and who did it, and he and other Whigs criticized financial mistreatment of them—when Democrats engaged in it.[21]

Clay supported another proposed migration of people of color: colonization of free Black Americans in Africa, which he and Lincoln saw as a solution to slavery. Clay was cofounder and later president of the American Colonization Society. Lincoln's first known public reference to colonization came in his eulogy for Clay in 1852. Speaking in 1855 to the Illinois State Colonization Society, he discussed possible costs, but not that the federal government spent large sums to force Native Americans westward. From the time of Africans arriving in 1619, colonists and their descendants were willing to migrate or make others do so. Colonization reflected this willingness, as did Indian removal. If Lincoln and Clay could encourage African Americans to leave the continent where they had lived for generations, they could force Native Americans to migrate from where they had lived for thousands of years.[22]

Like Clay, Lincoln sought the middle ground on most issues, but he discerned that in partisan politics some battles were unwinnable. In 1838, in his first antislavery statement at the Illinois legislature, Lincoln said that slavery was "founded on both injustice and bad policy; but that the promulgation of abolition doctrines tends rather to increase than to abate its evils." In 1844, after the antislavery Liberty Party won enough votes in New York to cost Clay the presidential election after he waffled on Texas, Lincoln wrote, "If the whig abolitionists of New York had voted with us last fall, Mr. Clay would now be president, whig principles in the ascendent, and Texas not annexed; whereas, by the division, all that either had at stake in the contest, was lost." In addition to slavery, abolitionists fought Indian removal, which they blamed on slaveholders seeking to expand their empire. If Lincoln disliked removal, even with its links to slavery, he appears to have remained silent about it.[23]

Nor did Lincoln's ambitions encourage such stands. Territorial and state officials had debated whether to permit slavery in Illinois and to allow free black people to live there; other Illinoisans showed no sympathy for Native Americans whose land they wanted. Lincoln opposed slavery, but given the political climate in his state and elsewhere, kept that largely to himself. If he felt strongly, speaking out against mistreatment of Indigenous peoples would have been uncharacteristic and politically unwise.[24]

### Whiggery and a Wife

Although unable to vote or campaign openly, Mary Todd shared her husband's ideology and love for politics, and it helped inspire their courtship and, finally, marriage on November 4, 1842. She grew up in a Whig family; her father Robert was an ally of Clay, who lived nearby. Politics helped bring together the Lincolns, and she felt free to express her views to him. They had something else in common: how Native Americans affected their ancestors and, ultimately, the Lincolns.[25]

In 1782 John Todd died in the Battle of Blue Licks, near present-day Mount Olivet, Kentucky. American and Canadian Loyalists who crossed the Ohio River into Kentucky and hundreds of Native Americans killed most of a small group of militiamen. The region's senior army commander, George Rogers Clark, then gathered about a thousand men and destroyed five Shawnee villages, but no Indians died; they had left rather than face a larger force.[26]

Todd had been a leading figure in early Kentucky. Pennsylvania-born, he was one of Lexington's first settlers and left ample property to his daughter Mary Owen Todd. He stipulated that after his last living heir died, his brothers Levi and Robert would receive the land. When a fire leveled Fayette County's courthouse, it destroyed the only copy of John Todd's will. His daughter Mary married Robert Wickliffe, and after she died, the Todd family, including John's brother Robert, sued Wickliffe for the land. When Robert died during the trial, one of his heirs became involved: his daughter Mary Lincoln, whose husband joined the lawyers representing the family. The local district court ruled against them because no will existed, and the Kentucky Court of Appeals agreed. Just as Thomas Lincoln ended up unable to own any of his father's land and lost his Kentucky holdings, the Todd family ran into similar issues.[27]

The lawsuit and her background may have shaped what, if anything, Mary Lincoln thought of Native Americans. She may have affected Lincoln's views on African Americans: she grew up with slaves; her relatives opposed the spread of slavery in Kentucky; and her father agreed with Clay on colonization. Whatever she thought of her family's encounters with Indians, and their impact, Mary seems likely to have shared her opinions with him.[28]

### Lincoln, Native Americans, and Politics

When Lincoln discussed Indians, Whig partisanship outweighed his feelings about them or their treatment. Responding to Democrat Stephen Douglas's defense of Van Buren during the 1840 campaign, Lincoln accused the president of overspending. To Douglas's claim that some costs came from buying land from Native Americans, Lincoln replied, "Now it happens that no such purchase was made during that year. It is true that some money was paid that year in pursuance of Indian treaties; but no more, or rather not as much as had been paid on the same account in each of several preceding years."[29]

Lincoln and Douglas also argued about the Seminole War of 1835–42. When Douglas claimed the war increased federal spending, Lincoln countered, "This is true, and it is also true that during that and every other year that that war has existed, it has cost three or four times as much as it would have done under an honest and judicious administration of the Government." Jackson and Van Buren, he said, spent "foolishly, not to say corruptly." He cited a "fact . . . not found in the public reports," but from "the verbal statement of an officer of the navy, who says he knows it to be true": When federal officials required a steamboat, the owner offered to sell it for $10,000. Instead, they rented it for $100 a day. Thus, they spent $92,000 and used it for three years—approximately the war's length when Lincoln spoke.[30]

Yet Lincoln praised thriftiness in connection with an act that is now widely condemned. "Again, Mr. Douglass [*sic*] says that the removal of the Indians to the country west of the Mississippi created much of the expenditure of 1838," Lincoln said. But public documents showed decreased spending. "For this small sum, altho' we do not think the administration entitled to credit, because large sums have been expended in the same way in former years, we consent it may take one and make the most of it," he said and later lauded Winfield

Scott's handling of that removal: the Trail of Tears. Scott was a Whig, and that was good enough for Lincoln.[31]

In the 1848 election, Lincoln and the Whigs backed the nomination of General Zachary Taylor, a hero of the Mexican-American War who had been involved in Indian wars. Democrats chose Cass, who rose to brigadier general in the War of 1812 and, as secretary of war, oversaw operations during the Black Hawk War in Illinois in 1832 and the planning for the Trail of Tears. The antislavery Free-Soil Party opted for Martin Van Buren, the president during the Trail of Tears.[32]

During the campaign, Lincoln made a speech in the House that promoted his candidate and satirized his opponent and himself. Whatever his pride in his Black Hawk War service, Lincoln disparaged his military background and accused Cass of making too much of his own. In addition to poking fun at the Democrat's claims, Lincoln told his colleagues—and *Congressional Globe* readers—"If he saw any live, fighting indians, it was more than I did; but I had a good many bloody struggles with the musquetoes; and, although I never fainted from loss of blood, I can truly say I was often very hungry."[33]

Lincoln's political interest in Native Americans continued after the election. With Taylor in office, Lincoln viewed the Bureau of Indian Affairs as a patronage machine. In 1850 he informed Taylor's secretary of the interior, Thomas Ewing, of rumors about appointing his friend Dr. Anson Henry "to some Indian Agency. I wish now merely to say that of all those whom I have desired should receive appointments from this Administration, Dr. Henry was at first, has always been, and still is, No. One with me." Whether Henry was qualified, interested in, or humanitarian toward Native Americans was immaterial.[34]

That seemed to sum up Lincoln the Whig: always a politician, but when he could have gained political traction through attacks on Native Americans (or total silence on slavery), he did not. When trying to aid Henry and eulogizing Taylor and Clay in the early 1850s, Lincoln was in the political wilderness, without prospects of advancement in a predominantly Democratic state. The Kansas-Nebraska Act, as he put it, "aroused me again" and seven years after his old rival Douglas introduced the measure, Lincoln had rocketed to the presidency.[35]

That followed his migration to the Republican Party, which, like the Whigs, evinced little interest in Native Americans. The party's 1856 and 1860 platforms ignored them. In the 1850s Lincoln's only allusion to them after his Taylor eulogy was in his first lecture on discoveries and inventions in 1858, when he referred to a "savage" who might learn from an animal about how to ford a stream, but even that left open what period he was discussing or who the savage would have been.[36]

But what Lincoln and the Republican Party stood for and the fate of Native Americans mingled more than any of those involved may have grasped. The party's ideology of free labor meant a commitment to opportunity—the belief, as Lincoln said in 1859, "that there is no such thing as a freeman being fatally fixed for life, in the condition of a hired laborer." Lincoln's rise from poor farm boy to middle-class lawyer and political leader exemplified this statement, as did the party's opposition to the spread of slavery and the belief, as Lincoln put it, in "the God-given rights to enjoy the fruits of their own labor." But he said, "If any continue through life in the condition of the hired laborer, it is not the fault of the system, but because of either a dependent nature which prefers it, or improvidence, folly, or singular misfortune." Asking who was "dependent," Eric Foner wrote, "The answer was provided by the course of development of American society itself," in a nation "whose westward expansion (the guarantee of equal opportunity) required the removal of Indians and the conquest of lands held by Mexicans."[37]

Indian removal long predated Lincoln's ascent but was connected to his ideology. The territory that Republicans wanted to keep free from slavery and open to free laborers—especially free white laborers—lay to the West. Native Americans lived on that land. The success of free labor and the party, including homesteading and a transcontinental railroad, required controlling that land and the people on it, or removing those people from it. On November 8, 1860, when the results came in, Lincoln learned the issue would be in his and his party's hands.

## PEOPLE, POLICY, AND BUREAUCRACY

Soon after taking office, Abraham Lincoln met Charles Francis Adams, the third generation of his family to be minister to England. When Secretary of State William Henry Seward brought him in, Adams thanked Lincoln, who replied, "Very kind of you to say so, Mr. Adams, but you are not my choice. You are Seward's man." Then, happy to resolve a patronage matter, Lincoln said, "Well, Seward, I have settled the Chicago post office." Adams wrote, "The man is not equal to the hour." By contrast, one scholar noted, "The country had just fallen apart; now was precisely the time to cement the remainder with patronage."[1]

As the first Republican president, following a Democrat whose administration included secessionists who left their jobs, Lincoln had ample patronage to give; as president during the Civil War, he had much to deal with. In his first year, he addressed issues and crises as an experienced politician but inexperienced leader. He grew accustomed to his office, but politics remained critical. Native Americans were less of a priority than slavery, the war, and the Union but played an important role in his administration's actions, and their fate intertwined with that of the Union. Indeed, patronage and policies affecting them proved inseparable from the rest of the Union war effort, and from the corruption and reform that characterized the Republican Party.

### The Men in Charge

Lincoln and other leading Republicans gave little reason to hope for changes in federal Indian policy. Their 1856 and 1860 platforms ignored Indigenous people, as would Lincoln's reelection platform in 1864. Seward had articulated a continental vision: while campaigning for Lincoln he said "the people of the great west" would determine the country's future, and Indian Territory, where the government drove the tribes in the Trail of Tears, "must be vacated." Secretary of War Simon Cameron earned the nickname "the Great Winnebago Chieftain" amid charges of cheating that group during treaty negotiations in the 1830s.[2]

Republicans were more inclined toward the Cameron approach. Their party's platform in 1860 attacked "the reckless extravagance which pervades every department of the Federal Government" and deemed "a return to rigid economy and accountability . . . indispensable to arrest the systematic plunder of the public treasury by favored partisans." But as a Minnesota Republican said, "How pleasant to think of, and how delightful to enjoy are those nice fat offices that our generous Uncle has provided." Lincoln sought competence, but in choosing his Cabinet and "political generals" he hoped to unite his party's factions, and the North. And his appointees had friends and allies seeking jobs.[3]

As in other posts, Lincoln's choices for the key positions for Native American affairs reflected his emphasis on party loyalty and usefulness, not in-depth knowledge of policy or those it affected. Onetime Whig lawmaker Caleb Smith's reward for steering Indiana's delegation to Lincoln at the 1860 convention was the Interior Department; another Indiana delegate, John Usher, was his deputy and then successor. Illinois Republican William Dole became commissioner of Indian Affairs. Like most of their predecessors, they neither knew nor cared much about Native Americans but valued connections: Usher engineered deals with the Union Pacific Railroad while in office and then worked for the company, and a Republican editor claimed Smith "was another Indian contract jobber," and Dole "intrigued for himself (in thieving Indian contracts)." Indeed, Dole provided jobs to family members and a later congressional probe raised questions about his actions.[4]

Another Illinoisan played a role in federal action: John Nicolay. A German immigrant and editor who became Lincoln's secretary,

Nicolay took several trips west on Indian matters, including the Dakota uprising in Minnesota in 1862, prompting fellow secretary John Hay to ask, "Where is your scalp?" Nicolay called war "the normal condition of savage life" and disdained the Native American's "ineradicable habits of indolence and carelessness," and "improvidence and wastefulness." He and Hay idolized Lincoln but seem not to have influenced him. Lincoln believed in "Christianizing" Indians and could be condescending, but publicly and privately he was more tolerant than Nicolay.[5]

Between Lincoln being the first Republican president, secession, and the lack of civil service regulations, the personnel turnover proved significant. His reputation for honesty was one reason his party chose him over Thurlow Weed's partner in New York's political machine, Seward, whose nomination would have undermined Republican attacks on James Buchanan's corrupt administration. After the election, Republicans complained about Democrats embezzling funds set aside for Native Americans and encouraging Indians in the South to support the rebels. According to a *New York Herald* Washington reporter, "republicans in this vicinity believe Mr. Buchanan's officials capable of almost everything in the way of malfeasance. . . . No change to the better is expected previous to the inauguration of 'Honest Old Abe.'"[6]

Little changed after that, either. On local patronage, Lincoln followed tradition, deferring to congressmen who put loyalty first. Examples of venality abounded: A Colorado agent received two paychecks while living in a house far from his jurisdiction, and another became 1,700 percent wealthier than he was when he took a $1,000-a-year job two years earlier. When Oregon's superintendent reported corruption, his state's congressmen asked Usher to fire him; Usher tried but Lincoln, possibly sensing that they benefited from it, said no.[7]

Low pay contributed to the problem. With $2,000 annually for superintendents and $1,500 for agents, one commentator noted, "To tempt any really capable person to leave home and civilized resorts for a life among savages, something more was required than a salary less than is paid to a first-class clerk in a dry goods store." Appointees agreed they could supplement their salaries through graft that helped their friends or defrauded those they were supposed to serve.[8]

Lincoln heard about some of these problems, but how closely he listened and what he felt he could do about them are debatable. With Dakota Territory agency supervisor Walter Burleigh accused of fraud, Lincoln told Dole, "I think you should suspend his official functions until these charges be heard, and that the charges be brought to a hearing as soon as possible"—an easier request for a territorial official than a state with congressmen. Dole did his best to protect Burleigh, who reputedly paid him off. Congress investigated and found wholesale corruption—but by then Dakota Territory had elected Burleigh as its House delegate. Nor was Burleigh alone: Dole, Usher, and Nicolay profited when the administration sold Sac and Mesquakie land in Kansas.[9]

Clearly, Lincoln should have known better. Indeed, in Washington Territory, his supporters were so pervasive that they were called "the Tribe of Abraham." The territory's seven Indian agents included two of his Illinois friends and two Oregon businessmen who used the job to help their land and mining speculation. Anson Dart, another appointee, lost his post when the administration learned that he bribed an Oregon politician to recommend him. In central Washington, one agent sold provisions meant for the Yakama.[10]

Washington Territory's problems went beyond patronage. When the administration, seeking Democratic support, chose longtime resident Benjamin Kendall as superintendent, Republicans felt betrayed. Worse, Kendall angered Anson Henry, an old friend and ally whom Lincoln named the territory's surveyor-general, enabling him to scour the landscape for ore. Accusing Kendall of fraud, he groused, "He not only refused every man I had suggested to him, but removed the very men I had urged him to retain." Henry warned Dole that Kendall could cost Republicans the Pacific Northwest.[11]

Several issues, none meant to benefit Natives, affected the result. Kendall removed Nez Perce Reservation teaching supervisor James Wilbur, a Methodist missionary who obtained jobs for two relatives and tried to force Catholic converts to give up that faith. Linking his actions to Oregon politics, Henry told Lincoln that Kendall had "grossly insulted" Oregon's Methodists, "the main prop of the Republican & Union cause, not only of that State, but of the whole

Pacific Coast." Democrats might win the next Oregon Senate race, but, he wrote, "Should you conclude to remove him, I think you will be Entirely safe in allowing Our Delegate to name his successor." Henry won. Wilbur returned to the reservation and hectored Nez Perce who refused to renounce Catholicism. Kendall started a newspaper that battled a publication Henry controlled, and one of Henry's associates eventually shot and killed Kendall.[12]

Nor did matters improve when Lincoln knew the appointees themselves. James Short, a friend from New Salem, ran into financial troubles both in Illinois and after relocating to California. Lincoln named him Round Valley Indian Reservation agent under another Illinoisan, superintendent George Hanson, who sought reforms, fired several Bureau of Indian Affairs employees, and suspended Short on charges of gambling and living with a pair of Native women.[13]

The corruption also involved those wielding the patronage. A mining company representative with ties to congressmen became Arizona's territorial superintendent of Indian affairs. Senator Samuel Pomeroy of Kansas had negotiated a treaty with the Potawatomie and emerged with ninety thousand acres of land (and another fifty thousand acres from the Kickapoo for a railroad he controlled). Senator Morton Wilkinson of Minnesota sought $50,000 for a Winnebago reservation for "improvements," hoping for "a chance to employ our friends." Later he directed federal funds to an ally's company to sell off Winnebago land. Lincoln's Republicans could be as corrupt toward Native Americans as their predecessors had been and their successors would be.[14]

### Reform and Lincoln's Men

A key part of the Republican Party's origins can become obscured: as opponents of slavery, its founders belonged to an "age of reform" that included expanded suffrage and women's rights. Not all reformers were Republicans, nor were all Republicans part of movements: Lincoln criticized abolition and temperance advocates, yet opposed slavery and avoided alcohol. Republicans felt less strongly about Indian reform, which still paralleled other crusades: reformers often disagreed and presumed to know what was best for the intended beneficiaries.[15]

But advocates and politicians often clashed. When Democrat James Polk beat Henry Clay in the 1844 election, Lincoln explained that if antislavery Whigs, upset with Clay waffling on annexing Texas, had voted for him instead of the Liberty Party, they would have accomplished more. An abolitionist told him, "We are not to do evil that good may come." He replied, "An evil tree can not bring forth good fruit. If the fruit of electing Mr. Clay would have been to prevent the extension of slavery, could the act of electing have been evil?" Instead they wound up with Texas and "could have prevented it, without a violation of principle, if they had chosen." As president, he said of Radical Republicans late in 1863, "They are nearer to me than the other side, in thought and sentiment, though bitterly hostile personally. They are utterly lawless—the unhandiest devils in the world to deal with—but after all their faces are set Zionwards." Reformers, he found, could be useful to his purposes.[16]

Administration officials grasped the existing system's faults and seemed to agree on a response. In his first annual message, Lincoln discussed problems in Indian Territory, Kansas, and New Mexico. In the Interior Department section, Smith noted that Kansas, Nebraska, and Old Northwest tribes were "gradually progressing in the arts of civilization," meaning an increased commitment to farming; Native Americans had done that for generations but not to the exclusion of other activities like hunting, which white settlement made difficult. Smith said, "A continuance of this policy, by familiarizing them with the habits of agricultural life, will gradually lead them to depend upon the cultivation of the soil for subsistence" and thus to give up their culture.[17]

Smith also voiced the combination of his party's reform tendencies and the disdain for Native peoples that so many Americans shared. Calling them "incompetent to manage their own business, or to protect their rights in their intercourse with the white race," he stressed that the government needed to act on their behalf. He criticized those who abused them. His proposed solutions included barring Indian agents from licensing traders, amending old treaties, and writing new ones to make payments in the form of "goods and agricultural implements."[18]

Expanding on Smith's comments, Dole urged a stronger reservation system and assimilation. "As the ultimate object of all our operations among the Indians should be to better their condition," the government must "endeavor to secure for them reservations of such dimensions, and possessing such natural facilities in climate, soil, and all other desirable qualities, as will, so far as possible, remove the obstacles in the way of their advancement, and present to them the greatest inducements to abandon savage and adopt civilized modes of life." Also, this would protect the Native from "vices and temptations . . . to which he seems to have an almost irresistible inclination."[19]

A year later, Smith and Dole still urged concentration while presaging discussions of African Americans in uniform. Noting Native Americans serving in Indian Territory, Dole welcomed "the highest praise to their soldierly bearing in battles, in camp, and upon the march." If anything, Dole was more doubtful about those moving onto their lands: they remained "the objects of the cupidity of their white neighbors." He set a goal of "their ultimate admission to all the rights of citizenship, as from time to time the improvement and advancement made by a given tribe may warrant . . . and would, I doubt not, prove a powerful incentive to exertion on the part of the Indians themselves."[20]

By 1863 Usher succeeded Smith, but the policies and condescension continued. Dole stated his party's attitude: "The object of all our efforts in behalf of the Indian should be the improvement of his condition." But Dole and Native Americans defined the terms differently. He declared, "The plan of concentrating Indians and confining them to reservations may now be regarded as the fixed policy of the government. The theory of this policy is doubtless correct," but "grave errors," especially creating smaller reservations, exposed Indigenous people to Anglo wiles and dangers. He expanded on his solution: severalty, long before Henry Dawes, a Republican congressman during the Civil War, pushed through the law designed to achieve it. The problem, he said, had been giving the land to members of a tribe "without regard to the disposition of the allottee to occupy the land allotted him, his previous good conduct, or his ability to cultivate or derive any benefit." Instead, Dole argued, "make the allotment of a tract of land to the Indian a special mark of the favor and approbation of his 'Great Father,' on account of his good conduct, his industry, and his disposition to abandon the ancient customs of his tribe, and engage in the more rational pursuits of civilization."[21]

Dole kept seeking concentration. White people mistreated Indians, but he saw it as "fully corroborated by our past history, that the white and the red man cannot occupy territory in common." Thus the need "for each race a separate abiding-place," which reeked of the case for black colonization or the racial separation that many Republicans preferred. Dole proposed up to five reservations nationally on public land to promote "the security of our frontier settlements, and the ultimate reclamation and civilization, and consequently the permanent welfare, of the Indians." The order of his priorities was no coincidence.[22]

Other Republicans debated the government's policies and lamented numerous accounts of corruption and incompetence. *The New York Times*, often an administration voice, backed concentration. In January 1863 a *Times* editorial lamented, "The Government, with praiseworthy intention, has organized a system intended to secure the exercise of a patriarchal supervision, while it leaves the different tribes in possession of national independence. . . ." But instead of "increasing in numbers and improving in moral and social condition . . . they dwindle away and degenerate," the *Times* said. Their land proved "productive of no benefit to themselves. . . . Close contact with the eager pioneers generates demoralization and decay." Endorsing "colonization and condensation," the *Times* would gather "the semi-civilized Indians of the Western States . . . into a homogenous community, where they can be isolated from the whites, and successfully instructed in the arts of agriculture and mechanics, and the higher principles of Christianity."[23]

But in one sarcastic editorial, the *Times* also questioned federal actions. It noted Dole's warning that ten thousand Native Americans at a Kansas fort, with $500,000 already appropriated "to keep them peaceable," would "give us much trouble" unless "enlisted to fight for the Union." Dole "goes to the 'Great Father' Abraham, procures several millions of dollars, and rushes to the rescue. He scatters greenbacks among the bronzed braves, and forthwith the crisis is past!" The *Times* wondered "what rich *sutler-ships* will grow out of the organization— what contracts for food and transportation—what a margin for profit between habitual dog-soup and hypothetical salt pork!" The *Times* also reported on malfeasance affecting Indigenous refugees in Kansas and demanded investigations, which led nowhere.[24]

## Reformers and Lincoln

Concentrating different tribes on large reservations and separating them from Anglo settlers seemed reasonable to many Republicans, but reformers sought deeper changes. They were few in number, with the Indian Rights movement still embryonic; a truly vocal effort awaited the postwar era. But two stood out: John Beeson and Henry Whipple.

Whipple became involved in reform as the war approached. Touring Minnesota after becoming its Episcopal bishop in 1859, he saw Native Americans as victims of oppression and corruption. With federal agents serving themselves, not their charges, Whipple urged reform and predicted the Dakota revolt two years before it happened. He reached out to federal and local officials, to no avail.[25]

So Whipple went to the top. Writing to Lincoln in March 1862, he proposed a study commission, education programs, and replacing annuity payments with products that Natives needed rather than funds the traders and agents could steal. He told Lincoln, "The Indian must have a home; his wandering tribal relations must be broken up; he must be furnished with seed, implements of husbandry, and taught to live by the sweat of his brow"—in other words, what Dole sought. But Whipple saw the Bureau itself as needing reform. Neither Lincoln, distributing patronage to build support, nor Dole, the Bureau's head, seemed likely to agree. But Lincoln wrote, "I have the honor to acknowledge the receipt of your esteemed favour of the 6th of March and to state in reply that I have commended the matter of which it treats to the special attention of the Secretary of the Interior."[26]

Whipple kept trying. He thanked Lincoln for referring him to Smith and returned to the subject of corruption, which neither Lincoln nor the Minnesota politicians he corresponded with had much, if any, desire to address. Arguing that Native Americans needed a system of governance and law, Whipple displayed his displeasure with federal officials and doubts about tribal leadership. In turn, Smith reported Congress would have to act for any changes to ensue and endorsed concentration.[27]

Seeking a private meeting with Lincoln, Whipple used connections. His cousin, Henry Halleck, became general-in-chief a few months after Whipple's first letter to Lincoln. His fellow Episcopalian Salmon Chase, the secretary of the treasury, provided an introductory letter. The bishop came to Lincoln's office on September 15, 1862. In the months since their correspondence, the Dakota had fulfilled Whipple's prediction of an uprising.[28]

Whipple made the most of his chance. He discussed how Native Americans lived, detailed Bureau graft, and urged reforms. Whipple recalled that Lincoln had told him a story: "Bishop, a man thought that monkeys could pick cotton better than negroes could because they were quicker and their fingers smaller. He turned a lot of them into his cotton field, but he found that it took two overseers to watch one monkey. It needs more than one honest man to watch one Indian agent." Beyond displaying an understanding of the corruption, Lincoln may have employed his technique of using humor to deflect critics and questions. But Whipple said Lincoln vowed, "If we get through this war, and I live, this Indian system shall be reformed."[29]

This meeting's results—and lack of them—were striking. Whipple told Halleck, "You have his ear. Do, for the sake of the poor victims of a nation's wrong, ask him to put on it something better than politicians." But Halleck seems to have shown no interest, and his performance as general-in-chief suggests consistency in his detachment. Lincoln gave Whipple an official card and directed Smith to let him examine Interior Department archives; Whipple studied treaties with the Dakota but had no further interactions with Lincoln or his administration. And by telling Whipple the war came first, Lincoln bought time or avoided the issue. A few weeks after meeting Whipple, his annual message to Congress included the diffident sentences: "I submit for your especial consideration whether our Indian system shall not be remodelled. Many wise and good men have impressed me with the belief that this can be profitably done." But that was all; he offered no specifics.[30]

Nor did action follow. Two weeks after Lincoln's message, the Union lost at Fredericksburg and Senate Republicans tried to oust Seward; although the government still functioned, other issues demanded attention. Then the Dakota uprising culminated in a mass execution, which Minnesotans at home and in Congress applauded, and a mass commutation, which made them angry at Lincoln. Out of partisanship, love of patronage, or lack of interest, congressmen made no effort to change the system as Whipple urged or Lincoln proposed.[31]

Lincoln kept encouraging reform, but tentatively. "I suggested in my last annual message the propriety of remodelling our Indian system. Subsequent events have satisfied me of its necessity," he wrote in December 1863. "Sound policy and our imperative duty to these wards of the government demand our anxious and constant attention to their material well-being, to their progress in the arts of civilization, and, above all, to that moral training which, under the blessing of Divine Providence, will confer upon them the elevated and sanctifying influences, the hopes and consolation of the Christian faith." His sentiments, like Dole's, mingled disrespect for Native Americans with a desire for their betterment. He and other Americans also showed that their priorities lay elsewhere. He promised to submit treaties that "contain stipulations for extinguishing the possessory rights of the Indians to large and valuable tracts of land. It is hoped that the effect of these treaties will result in the establishment of permanent friendly relations with such of these tribes as have been brought into frequent and bloody collision with our outlying settlements and emigrants," whose fate mattered more to Lincoln and his party.[32]

The lack of movement on reform, and Lincoln's desire to postpone it, was clear. Native Americans received no further attention; the main issue was his Reconstruction plan. Lincoln wanted "our Indian system . . . remodelled" and expected "reasonable success" for some reforms in California that Congress approved. But, he said, "much yet remains to be done to provide for the proper government of the Indians in other parts of the country to render it secure for the advancing settler, and to provide for the welfare of the Indian." He heard again from Whipple but took no action, referring him to William Windom, a congressman from Minnesota who supported removal. Ultimately, in 1864, Whipple gave up on Lincoln and voted for his old friend George McClellan.[33]

Beeson fared no better. An English-born abolitionist, he moved from Illinois to Oregon during the 1850s. Beeson so ardently defended Oregon's Indigenous people that public reaction forced him to leave the territory for a decade. He published the book *A Plea for the Indians* and a journal, both ahead of their time in calls for reform and criticism of the treatment of Native Americans.[34]

Beeson sought influence from the outset. When he asked Dole to name him special commissioner to Native peoples, Dole complained to a congressman that Beeson and other reformers had no understanding of the issues. Returning the contempt, Beeson told Lincoln that Dole's "lack of knowledge of Indian nature, and of human rights was shockingly manifested." He also praised Whipple despite disagreeing with him: Beeson advocated recognizing Native sovereignty and returning their land to them, which went beyond Whipple's reforms and was politically unpalatable. The abolitionist attacked white supremacy, declaring Native Americans had "as much capacity and as great desire for improvement as is possessed by the average of mankind." Beeson followed Whipple's example in meeting with Lincoln, in the summer of 1864. Beeson said that Lincoln told him, "My aged Friend. I have heard your arguments time and again. I have said little but thought much, and you may rest assured that as soon as the pressing matters of this war is [*sic*] settled the Indians shall have my first care and I will not rest untill Justice is done to their and to your satisfaction." He told Whipple much the same thing.[35]

Lincoln could not do the impossible, which reform may have been. Whipple told Dole that Indians needed not new treaties but "Christian manliness to fulfill old ones," and federal funds, assimilation, and Christian conversion would resolve many problems. But Smith told Whipple that congressmen would oppose reform so as to keep their patronage power and ability to profit from the system. Whipple heard that Secretary of War Edwin Stanton said, "What does the

Bishop want? If he came here to tell us that our Indian system is a sink of iniquity, tell him we all know it. Tell him the United States never cures a wrong until the people demand it; and when the hearts of the people are reached the Indian will be saved."[36]

At the same time, Lincoln confessed that Whipple "talked with me about the rascality of this Indian business until I felt it down to my boots," but he did little to push Congress. Indeed, he gave great latitude to Congress and his Cabinet. But he stepped in on some Indian issues, the military dealt with Native Americans regularly, and doing so affected the war effort. Lincoln had an excuse to act and chose not to use it. Perhaps he already had enough fights on his hands.[37]

### Indians, In Person

Perhaps Lincoln's failure to push reform also resulted from limited respect for Native peoples. A comparison with his views of African Americans is instructive. Frederick Douglass once said Lincoln "shared the prejudices common to his countrymen toward the colored race," but added, "in his company I was never in any way reminded of my humble origin or of my unpopular color." An African American "is not my equal in many respects—certainly not in color, perhaps not in moral or intellectual endowment," Lincoln said in 1858 in his first debate with Stephen Douglas. "But in the right to eat the bread . . . which his own hand earns, *he is my equal*" and "entitled to all the natural rights enumerated in the Declaration of Independence."[38]

Just as he understood the humanity of African Americans better than many of his contemporaries did, Lincoln seems not to have imbibed the malice that so many Americans, including his Uncle Mordecai, felt toward Native Americans. In an admittedly limited record, no evidence exists that he believed, as one of his generals allegedly said, that "the only good Indian I ever saw was dead." That sets a low standard. But one of Lincoln's personal encounters with Native Americans during the Civil War suggests a much lower opinion than he had of African Americans.[39]

On March 27, 1863, twelve Cheyenne, Kiowa, Arapaho, Comanche, Apache, and Caddo chiefs came to his office. Seward, Chase,

Secretary of the Navy Gideon Welles, New York War Democrat Daniel Dickinson, and Joseph Henry of the Smithsonian attended. Lean Bear (Cheyenne) and Spotted Wolf (Arapaho) made speeches through an interpreter. Lean Bear endorsed safe transit for white people across the plains and urged Lincoln "to counsel his white children, who were annually encroaching more and more upon tribes, to abstain from acts of violence and wrong toward them."[40]

Lincoln's response reflected a minimal understanding of Native peoples. After mentioning "the strange sights you see here, among your pale-faced brethren" and "the big wigwams," Lincoln said, "We pale-faced people think that this world is a great, round ball, and we have people here of the pale-faced family who have come almost from the other side of it to represent their nations here and conduct their friendly intercourse with us, as you now come from your part of the round ball." With a globe brought in, Lincoln said, "one of our learned men will now explain to you our notions about this great ball, and show you where you live." The chiefs, who knew they had traveled a considerable distance, then received a lecture from Henry, a news account said, about "the formation of the earth, showing how much of it was water and how much was land; and pointing out the countries with which we had intercourse. He also showed them the position of Washington and that of their own country, from which they had come."

One of Lincoln's comments apparently raised the chiefs' eyebrows. "Although we are now engaged in a great war between one another, we are not, as a race, so much disposed to fight and kill one another as our red brethren," he said. Despite cushioning the comment by referring to the Civil War, Lincoln managed to ignore other wars from around that globe he deemed so important for them to see.

Lincoln also discussed federal policies. "There is a great difference between this pale-faced people and their red brethren, both as to numbers and the way in which they live. We know not whether your own situation is best for your race, but this is what has made the difference in our way of living," he explained. "The pale-faced people are numerous and prosperous because they cultivate the earth, produce bread, and depend upon the products of the earth rather than wild game for a subsistence." Native Americans were divided over the value of farming, but the reservation system was intended to reduce hunting and how much land they used. He confessed that he was "not capable of advising you whether, in the providence of the Great Spirit, who is the great Father of us all, it is best for you to maintain the habits and customs of your race, or adopt a new mode of life. I can only say that I can see no way in which your race is to become as numerous and prosperous as the white race except by living as they do, by the cultivation of the earth," which ignored the size of the Native populace before white settlement.

But Lincoln also suggested some awareness and conscience. "It is the object of this Government to be on terms of peace with you, and with all our red brethren. We constantly endeavor to be so," he said. "We make treaties with you, and will try to observe them; and if our children should sometimes behave badly, and violate these treaties, it is against our wish. You know it is not always possible for any father to have his children do precisely as he wishes them to do." While this suggested he saw them as childlike in ways he did not regard African Americans, he showed that he knew the difficulties went far beyond the federal government's power. But he neither rectified the problem nor admitted that his administration joined in violating those treaties.

Clearly, Lincoln had a minimal understanding of Native peoples. David Nichols wrote, "There is no record of what went through the chiefs' minds at this incredible recitation by the president of the United States. . . . Lincoln managed to tie together the stereotype of the savage, nonfarming hunter with the inherently violent barbarian who was inferior to whites. Considering the bloodiness of the Civil War in 1863, it was a remarkable statement." Making it all the more remarkable, Lincoln had escaped the life of a subsistence farmer that his father led. He believed in the ability to rise through free labor that might involve agriculture but included other possibilities. He saw African Americans in those roles, even when he still supported colonization, but he apparently saw the Native case as far less hopeful.[41]

Another encounter similarly suggests his administration saw little reason to worry about a group lacking political power. In 1864 some

Kansas Indians arrived to negotiate a treaty. On July 8 Dole wrote to him, "Will you be kind enough to take these Indians by the hand this Evening[.] I wish them to start home by the early train in the morning." Whether Lincoln did is uncertain. That day he issued a proclamation on why he refused to sign a Reconstruction bill. Waging war, planning peace, and winning reelection mattered more to Lincoln than meeting with Native American visitors. That was understandable and consistent, and unfortunate. Many of the problems with Lincoln's Native American policies, and the difficulties he faced, no matter what direction he chose, were evident in Indian Territory.[42]

## THE PROBLEM WITH
## INDIAN TERRITORY

As the Civil War began, Abraham Lincoln and Jefferson Davis seemed mismatched: a one-term congressman and self-educated lawyer who joked about his brief militia service, and a West Pointer with vast government and military experience. The Confederacy's early success suggested Davis's superiority, and Indian Territory underscored why. Whereas Lincoln named Indiana Republican William Coffin superintendent in Kansas with authority over Indian Territory and appointed no agents for a year, Davis's government created an Indian Territory military district to underscore the area's importance, raised troops, negotiated with the "five civilized tribes," and annexed the area.[1]

How Lincoln originally addressed this issue suggests minimal interest in Native Americans and, especially in his first year, reflected the best and worst of his policies. Many historians have concentrated on the failings of larger armies elsewhere and ignored these developments. What happened in Kansas and Indian Territory revealed, as with the difficulties surrounding the eastern and western theaters, that the sure-handed leader of the war's later years was not yet in evidence.[2]

### "Our Wish Is for Peace"

Only about seventy thousand people lived in Indian Territory's nearly seventy thousand square miles in 1861. The Cherokee occupied the north, the Seminole a smaller central tract, the Creek much of the middle, and the Choctaw and Chickasaw most of its southland. The "Leased District" in the southwest had been Choctaw, but the United States paid them so it could locate other Native groups there. The area mattered less for its resources—notwithstanding Oklahoma's oil future—than as a potential buffer for the Union against Confederate invasions further west and for the rebels against a northern attack on Texas. Like Missouri, Kentucky, and Maryland, Indian Territory was a border area divided between the North and South and forced to choose between them.[3]

Indian Territory's residents had cause to distrust the Union and join the rebels. They were used to southern agents, the government had invested their annuities in southern funds, and rebel emissary Albert Pike offered better treaties than previous ones. In turn, Dole promised "the government would under no circumstances permit the smallest interference with their tribal or domestic institutions," meaning slavery, and he and Secretary of the Interior Caleb Smith assured veteran Cherokee leader John Ross of Union support.[4]

But they had heard similar promises before, and events and Union leadership conspired against the alliance. Pro-rebel agents, holdovers from James Buchanan, kept the Lincoln government's reassurances of support from reaching Indian Territory. Dole warned that Indigenous people there could succumb to southern persuasion and Smith sought military aid, but Lincoln had other concerns. Deeming them necessary elsewhere, the army pulled soldiers from the territory's three forts and Arkansas supply depot, violating treaties that protected the tribes, who felt abandoned. As the South sent troops and personal appeals and urged enlisting Cherokees, Ross awaited Union support. Although reputedly willing to ally with southerners, he told the rebels, "I am—the Cherokees are—your friends, but we do not wish to be brought into the feuds between yourselves and your Northern Brethren. Our wish is for peace. Peace at home and Peace among you."[5]

Ross eventually faced the inevitable. "A decided Union man," as the *New York Tribune* called him, he led one Cherokee faction; another was loyal to others, including his longtime rival Stand Watie, who rose to brigadier general in the Confederate army (the only

Native American to achieve such a rank on either side). Finally, surrounded by rebel troops, and with Stand Watie defeating the Union nearby, Ross allied with the South in August 1861. He had no choice. As another Cherokee leader, Ayuñadegi, said, "We were perplexed and embarrassed," accepting "the ravage and ruin of our country" or buying time until "deliverance might come from our friends in the Government of the United States."[6]

Ross's situation compelled Lincoln to act, but so did other factors. When Stand Watie attacked, Native Americans ran ahead of the rebels to Kansas as refugees, creating problems for a new state still reeling from the bloody 1850s, and for the administration. In southeast Kansas, Fort Roe proved to be lacking resources and unable to meet the needs of Indigenous people in the area.[7]

The government debated one solution to its refugee problem: letting Native people fight. When Minnesota Ojibwe Hole-in-the-Day tried to raise troops, an intermediary assured Secretary of War Simon Cameron that he "would undoubtedly, if accepted, be willing to conform to the usages of civilized warfare, as he is not a savage, but in many respects fully civilized and Christianized." Cameron replied, "You can say to him that the President as well as this Department is much pleased by his fidelity to the Government," but "the nature of our present national troubles, forbids the use of savages." Some Republicans disagreed: "It would require no persuasion to raise a large Indian force in Kansas and Nebraska to operate against those who may be brought into the field by the Rebels," the *New York Tribune* argued. Dole expected them to get "the same pay as other volunteers, whilst the chiefs will receive a higher remuneration." Soon after, General David Hunter sought "authority to muster into the service a Brigade of Kansas Indians to assist the Creeks, Seminoles, and Chickasaws."[8]

Lincoln's December 1861 message relegated Native Americans to a paragraph. He wrote, "The relations of the Government with the Indian tribes have been greatly disturbed by the insurrection, especially in the southern superintendency and . . . New Mexico. The Indian country south of Kansas is in the possession of insurgents from Texas and Arkansas." He explained the obstacles to sending loyal appointees into rebel territory to replace exponents of "the insurrectionary cause." Despite lacking "official information," he reported "several prominent chiefs" had assured Dole of their loyalty and a desire for "Federal troops to protect them." He suggested that "upon the repossession of the country by the Federal forces the Indians will readily cease all hostile demonstrations and resume their former relations to the Government." His administration's failure to act sooner went unmentioned.[9]

The Interior Department report to Congress echoed and expanded on Lincoln. Smith declared, "The spirit of rebellion against the authority of the government, which has precipitated a large number of States into open revolt, has been instilled into a portion of the Indian tribes by emissaries from the insurrectionary States." Smith implied Cabinet infighting: "It is unfortunate that the War Department has been unable to send to that region such a body of troops as would be adequate to the protection of those tribes, and revive their confidence in the ability as well as the will of the United States to comply with their treaty stipulations." After that, he expected them to "renounce all connexion with the rebel government and resume their former relations."[10]

Lincoln's decision to fight for Indian Territory in late 1861, and try to resolve the refugee crisis and political war in Kansas, was significant on several levels. A year before the Emancipation Proclamation made the same possible for African Americans, his action led to Native peoples joining the army. That once unimaginable step resulted from a need for personnel. In keeping with political fights involving generals, the quest to regain Indian Territory became intertwined with politics in Kansas and in Washington, DC.[11]

## "Judgment and Discretion"

Two men pushed Lincoln to enroll Native American soldiers. An Illinois businessman between army stints, General David Hunter had long opposed slavery. A onetime Indiana Democrat who voted for the Kansas-Nebraska Act, Kansas politician and aspiring general James Lane became ardently antislavery during the Bleeding Kansas border war and one of the new state's first U.S. senators in 1861. They agreed on the need to recruit soldiers of color—and on wanting to be rid of the other. The conflicts between generals, politicians, and political generals that annoyed and flummoxed Lincoln throughout the war also played out over and in Indian Territory.[12]

Lane sought to command a new military district that included Kansas and Indian Territory, then to attack rebels in Arkansas and Texas. Coffin backed Lane, as did Mark Delahay, a Lincoln ally from Illinois who had relocated to Kansas. They blamed the loss of the "large, beautiful and most fertile tract" of Indian Territory on southern leaders who used "falsehood . . . to array the aborigines" against the Union. They reminded Lincoln of the region's strategic value for fighting the western Confederacy and portrayed Lane as best-equipped to secure it.[13]

Instead, hoping the professional soldier would be more diplomatic and adept than the political Lane, Lincoln gave Hunter command. He told Cameron that he wanted Lane "appointed a Brigadier General of Volunteers, to report to Gen. Hunter, and to be so assigned to duty as not to be under, over, or in immediate contact with Gen. [James] Denver," a onetime Kansas commissioner of Indian Affairs, territorial secretary, and governor under James Buchanan. Denver and Lane had been foes, and Lincoln hoped to bring a War Democrat into the fold.[14]

But Hunter and Lane managed to vex Lincoln individually and together. Hunter's meetings with Native leaders neither regained land nor slowed the flow of refugees. Aware of Lane's importance and ambition, Lincoln suggested "judicious co-operation" and addressed Hunter as he did other generals, combining deference and authority with subtlety: "I propose to offer you a few *suggestions*, knowing how hazardous it is to bind down a distant commander in the field to specific lines and operations, as so much always depends on a knowledge of localities & passing events. It is intended, therefore, to leave a considerable margin for the exercise of your judgment and discretion."[15]

Judgment and discretion had limits, and Lincoln ordered Hunter to command an expedition to retake Indian Territory with Lane involved. The general replied that acting with so few men would be impossible—a complaint similar to George McClellan's about the

Army of the Potomac—and blamed Lane for pressuring Lincoln. The president tried to reason with Hunter, who claimed to be "deeply mortified, humiliated, insulted and disgraced" to be "in banishment" in the "wilderness" of Fort Leavenworth with fewer than three thousand men.[16]

Responding at the end of 1861 that it was hard "to answer so ugly a letter in good temper," Lincoln said, "I am, as you intimate, losing much of the great confidence I placed in you, not from any act or omission of yours touching the public service, up to the time you were sent to Leavenworth, but from the flood of grumbling despatches and letters I have seen from you since." Lincoln dismissed his "unwarranted assumption that the ordering you to Leavenworth must necessarily have been done as a *punishment* for some *fault*," and complaints about his army's size: "You constantly speak of being placed in command of only 3000. Now tell me, is not this mere impatience? Have you not known all the while that you are to command four or five times that many?" He told Hunter, "I have been, and am sincerely your friend; and if, as such, I dare to make a suggestion. I would say you are adopting the best possible way to ruin yourself. 'Act well your part, there all the honor lies.' He who does *something* at the head of one Regiment, will eclipse him who does *nothing* at the head of a hundred."[17]

Ultimately, Lincoln tried to placate all involved and maneuver them into doing as he wanted. Soon after his letter to Hunter, the order came from the War Department to enlist four thousand Native Americans from the Kansas and Missouri borderlands. Native Americans would receive the same pay and benefits as white soldiers, unlike future African American soldiers. Enrolling Indians appealed to Hunter, but he had no desire for Lane to receive a command. Making matters worse for Hunter, Dole visited and found a disaster: as Coffin described the refugees, "It is impossible for me to depict the wretchedness of their condition," including health problems and limited food and clothing.[18]

Unfortunately, Hunter and Lane concentrated more on their power struggle than on aiding refugees and defeating rebels. By then Lincoln had grown used to disputes involving generals and politicians.

Amid political pressure—Delahay wired about "concentrated public sentiment in favor of General Lane as the commander of expedition south[.] I do hope you will not allow any obstacle to hinder that result"—Lincoln informed new Secretary of War Edwin Stanton at the end of January 1862, "I have not intended and do not now intend that it shall be a *great exhausting affair*, but a snug, sober column of 10,000 or 15,000," not a vehicle for Lane to build a political machine. Lincoln tried to resolve the dispute: "General Lane has been told by me many times that he is under the command of General Hunter, and assented to it as often as told. It was the distinct agreement between him and me when I appointed him that he was to be under Hunter."[19]

Dole also pressed Lincoln on Lane's behalf. "I could not have been mistaken, in the fact, that it was contemplated at Washington, that Genl Lane, should command the expedition," he said. "I am at the same time aware that it was expected, that Genl Hunter, would willingly acquiesce, in this arrangement, he retaining the superior command, and superintending, the entire organization, of the expedition, and controlling all its movements, untill it entered the field." But he also claimed that Hunter and Lane got along.[20]

As the feuding went on, Lincoln lost patience—as he sometimes did over military politics. First, writing to Hunter and Lane, he made clear who was in charge: "My wish has been and is to avail the Government of the services of both General Hunter and General Lane, and, so far as possible, to personally oblige both. General Hunter is the senior officer and must command when they serve together; though in so far as he can, consistently with the public service and his own honor, oblige General Lane, he will also oblige me," Lincoln wrote. Putting the military man above the politician, he added, "If they cannot come to an amicable understanding, General Lane must report to General Hunter for duty, according to the rules, or decline the service," which he did, returning to the Senate. Hunter's tenure also proved brief: a month after his letter, Hunter went east to assume another post.[21]

Lincoln then backed another expedition to Indian Territory. He wanted to help the starving and freezing refugees; also, Kansans wanted them out of their state. Lane's pressure in the Senate helped compel Lincoln, but so did military possibilities. Early in March 1862, the Union won a battle at Pea Ridge, Arkansas, in which Native Americans fought for the South. But many Native Americans felt less inclined to join the rebels or fight outside of Indian Territory, where the tribes split between the North and South. Confederate commander Albert Pike, resenting the lack of aid from his superiors, resigned that summer.[22]

In late March 1862, the War and Interior departments issued orders responding to Lincoln's decision. They disagreed on how many Native Americans to enroll but agreed on the need to act. Adjutant General Lorenzo Thomas reported Lincoln's wish for two regiments to enter "Indian country, with a view to open the way for friendly Indians who are now refugees in Southern Kansas to return to their homes and to protect them there. Five thousand friendly Indians will also be armed to aid in their own protection and you will please furnish them with the necessary subsistence." With Hunter gone, Lane picked the expedition's leader, General James Blunt, who informed his superior, General John Schofield, "The Indian regiments are fast filling up with recruits."[23]

When the army moved three months later, it succeeded, though not because of Lincoln or its talents. The expedition's scope declined to five thousand soldiers, including three thousand Indians. Crucially, after Pea Ridge, the rebels shifted their forces, enabling the Union to enter Indian Territory largely uncontested. Native Americans faced the same problems as other southern soldiers: a lack of pay and provisions, prompting desertions. For his part, Ross declared his wish to be taken captive, and Interior officials—Coffin, Dole, and Smith—made clear they knew that he had allied with the South unwillingly. In Indian Territory, other officers mutinied against Lane's choice of commander, prompting white soldiers who preferred not to serve beside Native Americans to return to Kansas. The Indian soldiers left behind generally wanted to go home and many did. Meanwhile, most refugees remained in Kansas.[24]

As the Indians' suffering went on, the next campaign in late 1862 encountered many of the problems of the earlier one. While Lane waged political war, Kansans wanted the refugees gone but disagreed over how to accomplish that goal. Lane tried to recruit Native American and African American troops, sometimes with administration support. The refugees preferred to return to Indian Territory, but the War Department felt unable to spare soldiers to escort them and feared another mutiny if white troops assisted Indians. For his part, Smith noted three new regiments from among the refugees and lamented the War Department's refusal to keep them in Kansas. An effort to bring refugees in Missouri back to Indian Territory failed, with several dying on the way. They lacked food, and Stand Watie's raids relieved them of most of what federal officials provided. Lincoln knew the government had shifted large populations, and his colonization schemes showed his willingness to try it again. But his administration declined or failed to provide the military and material resources the refugees needed.[25]

## "The Multitude of Cares"

Amid efforts to regain Indian Territory, Lincoln had another personal encounter with a Native American: a meeting with Ross. In the late summer of 1862, Blunt advised Ross to see him, telling Lincoln, "I have no doubt as to the loyalty of the Ross Family and three fourths of the Cherokee people," and reminding him that Ross had avoided allying with the South as long as possible. Endorsing the Cherokee and perhaps trying to make Lincoln feel guilty, Blunt reported their hope "that our force might arrive in their country, and insure them protection, this hope failing them, they were compelled to the policy they adopted as a matter of necessity and self-preservation."[26]

In case Blunt failed to win over Lincoln, Delahay chimed in. Lauding Ross for holding out so long against the rebels, he said, "I have assured him that you would be very glad to see him at Washington, and that you will afford him and the loyal people of the Nation every reasonable protection in your power, assuring him that you feel a deep interest in the restoration of peace and order in his beautiful country." He also encouraged military action in Kansas, predicting that Native American soldiers could "enable the loyal people of the Nation to hold their country and also reclaim many who have been led estray [sic] in a very few months, at least this is the opinion of some of our best Military men," by whom he probably meant Lane and Blunt.[27]

Lincoln may have been less friendly than Delahay urged. After Smith reported his arrival, the president replied on September 11, "I will see Mr. Ross at 9 a.m. to-morrow, if he calls." Between the political fight in Kansas and the recent uprising by the Dakota Sioux in Minnesota, Lincoln may have been wary of discussing Native issues. Nonetheless, Ross thanked Dole for "the friendly interview with which I have been honored by yourself and the President."[28]

Welcoming or not, Lincoln asked Ross to write his requests. No stranger to American officials, broken promises, or politics, Ross replied quickly. The Cherokee Nation "maintained in good faith her relations toward the United States up to a late period and subsequent to the occurrence of the war," but "the want of that protection, civil and military," that the United States had promised and "overwhelming pressure" had forced his people, "for the preservation of their country and their existence," to ally with the South. They had "no other alternative," Ross argued. He noted that "as soon as the Indian Expedition marched into the Country the great mass of the Cherokee People rallied spontaneously" to the Union. "The withdrawal of that expidition [sic] and the reabandonment of that people and Country to the forces of the Confederate States leaves them in a position fraught with distress, danger and ruin." Ross sought military protection and recognition of treaty obligations, and a proclamation announcing these commitments.[29]

Lincoln responded slowly, carefully, and unsatisfactorily to Ross, but perhaps as well as he could at the time. "In the multitude of cares claiming my constant attention I have been unable to examine and determine the exact treaty relations between the United States and the Cherokee Nation." That statement seems gratuitous: Lincoln was wise enough to know Ross had a compelling argument. He added, "Neither have I been able to investigate and determine the exact state of facts claimed by you as constituting a failure of treaty obligation on our part, excusing the Cherokee Nation for making a treaty with a portion of the people of the United States in open rebellion against the government thereof." That was debatable, since Blunt and

Delahay vouched for Ross. But Lincoln tried to placate Ross: "This letter therefore, must not be understood to decide anything upon these questions. I shall, however, cause a careful investigation of them to be made. Meanwhile the Cherokee people remaining practically loyal to the federal Union will receive all the protection which can be given them consistently with the duty of the government to the whole country. I sincerely hope the Cherokee country may not again be over-run by the enemy; and I shall do all I consistently can to prevent it."[30]

The administration moved slowly. Late in September, Smith reported on an 1835 treaty, never superseded, that promised to "protect the Cherokee Nation from domestic strife and foreign enemies," which the Union failed to do. Nearly two weeks later, Lincoln wired Samuel Curtis, the Department of the Missouri's new commander: "I believe some Cherokee Indian Regiments, with some white forces operating with them, now at or near Fort-Scott, are within your Department, & under your command." Ross, he said, "is now here, an exile; and he wishes to know, and so do I, whether the force above mentioned, could not occupy the Cherokee country, consistently with the public service. Please consider and answer." Curtis replied, "My forces have driven the enemy to Pineville, near the Indian line. I yesterday ordered an advance, driving them into the Territory and beyond. I doubt the expediency of occupying ground so remote from supplies, but I expect to make rebels very scarce in that quarter pretty soon." Lincoln and Ross accepted Curtis's promise and premise, but restoring Indian Territory would take about two years.[31]

### Regaining Indian Territory

Lincoln's annual message in December 1862 reported on Indian Territory. Its tribes, he said, "renounced their allegiance to the United States, and entered into treaties with the insurgents. Those who remained loyal to the United States were driven from the country. The chief of the Cherokees has visited this city for the purpose of restoring the former relations of the tribe with the United States. He alleges that they were constrained, by superior force, to enter into treaties with the insurgents, and that the United States neglected to furnish the protection which their treaty stipulations required." Although others in his administration agreed that Ross had no choice, Lincoln resorted to the lawyerly "alleges." He may have deemed it the best word, or had doubts about Ross or a desire for more evidence.[32]

In the summer of 1863, as at Gettysburg and Vicksburg, the tide in Indian Territory turned. The Cherokee passed a law guaranteeing that "Negro and other slaves" would be "forever free." Union troops regained control of much of the area. But some Cherokee remained loyal to the rebels, whose raids under William Quantrill's command created problems for the Union and Native Americans.[33]

That December 8, Lincoln issued his Proclamation of Amnesty and Reconstruction, whose meaning for one group of people obscured its impact on another. He stipulated that when 10 percent of the 1860 voting populations in rebel states swore fealty to the Union, they would be "recognized as the true government of the State." In Indian Territory soldiers distributed copies to the tribes, hoping to persuade them to renounce the South. Most refused, and Curtis warned against "any and all conclusions against our Government as to future rights of Indians who made war upon us."[34]

Yet Curtis also demonstrated sympathy for the refugees. In February 1864 he told Lincoln that he had "traversed and skirted" their lands. They remained "massed as refugees" and "exceedingly anxious to return." He again suggested sending more troops. The refugees in Kansas continued to cause problems for Lincoln, who had no need for the resulting political fight, and the army, whose leaders doubted they could spare the resources to help them return home.[35]

Finally, Lane devised the solution: getting Congress to fund their trip home, and demanding that Lincoln spend the money. Granted, some of the difficulty lay beyond Lincoln's power: Confederate guerrillas still preyed there, requiring the Union Army's attention and complicating the refugees' return. But in 1864 about five thousand refugees traveled from Kansas to Indian Territory in a six-mile caravan, with more than sixteen thousand camped near Fort Gibson. But it was too late in the year for planting.[36]

That October Lincoln approved $200,000 to feed and clothe them, then asked Congress for more money. Little had changed: between

Quantrill's raids and Bureau of Indian Affairs mismanagement, the refugees had trouble obtaining and keeping what little they had. Dole's annual report declared that "it can be no wrong to either class that they should be required to receive within the limits of the country other tribes with whom they are on friendly terms." Eventually, he thought, all of the tribes in Kansas and Indian and Nebraska territories would "become one people." As historian Mary Jane Warde observed, "Dole apparently believed the Indian nations' opinions, sovereignty, and identity to be as disposable as their land titles."[37]

### "An Unprovoked War"

Whether Lincoln's death affected the ultimate situation in Indian Territory is debatable. James Harlan, his choice to replace Usher as secretary of the interior in 1865, showed none of the shrewdness or kindness that might have been expected of the president who selected him. Nor did Dole remain at Indian Affairs after Lincoln's death; his replacement, Dennis Cooley, was a veteran of business and law who moved in lockstep with Harlan. Although several officials showed they grasped why the Cherokee allied with the rebels, Harlan still accused them of "flagrant violation of treaties which had been observed by us with scrupulous good faith" and of fighting "an unprovoked war upon us." Harlan wanted the Five Nations to cede land to which the federal government could move Native Americans from other areas.[38]

Although the Civil War may no longer have included military battles, fighting went on in Indian Territory within and between tribes, who resumed their old disputes. Later in 1865 Cooley informed them that fighting for the Confederacy had cost them their land and annuities. They would have to negotiate new treaties, free remaining slaves, give up more land, and consolidate into one territorial government. What Andrew Johnson's administration opposed in the South, it tried to do in Indian Territory. Treaties signed in 1866 and 1867 abolished slavery there, granted amnesty to those who sided with the rebels, assured the right-of-way to railroads, and allotted each Native American 160 acres of land, much as the Dawes Severalty Act would do two decades later.[39]

Whether Lincoln would have done better is debatable. Although he moved slowly, he did try to help the people he had done so little to assist before. Indian Territory residents wanted to stay in the Union or required little convincing to do so, but they received no encouragement early in his administration. Then their fate became intertwined with politics in the military and in Kansas. In response Lincoln tried to induce others to act before he would step in and to avoid becoming involved in local disputes. To say he should have been more involved is reasonable, especially with Native lives at stake, but the same could be said of other situations throughout the Union. Perhaps the Kansas refugees and Indian Territory mattered less to him and to his party than white men or slaves or free black people; perhaps the others simply mattered more.

Ma-Ka-Tai-Me-She-Kia-Kiah, or Black Hawk, who led the Sauk and
Mesquakie in the war where Lincoln "fought many bloody struggles with
the musquetoes." By then Black Hawk was an established warrior and
political leader, and this lithograph from a portrait shows him after the
war he had hoped to avoid. Library of Congress; LCCN 2013645340.

Black Hawk War—Battle of Bad Axe. On August 2, 1832, Black Hawk's followers tried to cross the Mississippi and "to give themselves up—the whites paid no attention to their entreaties—but commenced *slaughtering* them!" Library of Congress; LCCN 2007683614.

Caleb Smith, who, like Lincoln, migrated from the Whigs to the Republicans. After he helped secure the Indiana delegation for Lincoln at the 1860 convention, his reward was to be secretary of the interior. Library of Congress; LCCN 2018669627

Photo, by Mathew Brady, of the delegation of Indigenous leaders who came to the White House and received a lecture about the globe. Lincoln's secretary John Nicolay, who had been in Minnesota the previous summer at the height of the Dakota uprising, is in the back row, center, with interpreter John Simpson Smith at the left in the back. Library of Congress; LCCN 2004669812.

Major General David Hunter, at about the time he fought Senator James Lane for control of the expedition to Indian Territory. Library of Congress; LCCN 98519152.

James Lane, whom Bleeding Kansas turned into a Radical Republican. Lane tried to turn Kansas into his political fiefdom, including dealing with Indigenous refugees and fighting to rid Indian Territory of Confederates. Library of Congress; LCCN 2017895718.

Chief John Ross, the longtime Cherokee leader, about a decade before he found that the Lincoln administration had left him no alternative but to ally with the Confederacy. Library of Congress; LCCN 2004664594.

James H. Carleton, who helped feed Utes but also prompted the Diné's version of the Trail of Tears, the Long Walk, by forcing them to move to Bosque Redondo. Library of Congress; LCCN 2018670232.

Delegation of Cheyenne and Arapaho leaders, including Black Kettle, who met on September 28, 1864, in Denver with Governor John Evans and Colonel John Chivington. Second from the left in the front row, Black Kettle told Evans and Chivington that "we have made peace." Two months later Chivington's troops slaughtered a large number of the Cheyenne and Arapaho people at Sand Creek. National Anthropological Archives, Smithsonian Institution; NAA INV 00388800.

*The Sand Creek Massacre.* This 1936 oil painting by Robert Lindneaux, created as part of the New Deal's Works Progress Administration, depicts the battle scene at Sand Creek, including, right of center, the flagpole with both an American flag and a white surrender flag, which Black Kettle thought demonstrated his peaceful intentions. History Colorado–Denver, Colorado.

# LINCOLN AND THE DAKOTA

When Abraham Lincoln approved hanging thirty-eight men for their part in the Dakota uprising in Minnesota in the summer of 1862, it was America's largest execution ever. But he threw out 264 death sentences—America's largest commutation ever. These events and their contradictory nature resulted from decades of policy, the impact of the Civil War, and Lincoln himself. Afterward Republicans criticized the commutations, which speaks to public opinion on Native peoples and the limits Lincoln faced if he tried to reform Indian policy.[1]

## "Let Them Eat Grass"

Minnesota's Native population long suffered at federal, state, and local hands. Four treaties from 1837 to 1858 reduced its property and forced the Dakota into an area on the Minnesota River about ten miles wide and 150 miles long. Pressured to engage in farming and manual labor as white settlement grew, Dakota leaders saw no choice but to accede, but a large number of Minnesota's Indians refused.[2]

Other problems plagued the Dakota before and during the Civil War. Thieves from outside their community raided agency storehouses. Traders swindled them and sold them alcohol illegally. Wartime dislocation and fiscal issues slowed annuity payments. One agent said of the Dakota that when he criticized them for fighting longtime enemies, they replied, "Our Great Father, we know, has always told us it was wrong to make war; now he is making war and killing a *great many*; how is this? We don't understand it."[3]

After a difficult winter in 1861, Native Americans needed food, but war and graft hamstrung them. Dakota leader Little Crow tried to work with federal officials, often to his followers' displeasure, and his latest failed effort had major consequences. He told trader Andrew Myrick, "We have waited a long time. The money is ours, but we cannot get it. We have no food, but here are these stores filled with food." But traders would do nothing without pay. Myrick said, "So far as I am concerned, if they are hungry let them eat grass or their own dung."[4]

Federal officials did little in response. In Minnesota, Lincoln left patronage to Republicans like Senator Morton Wilkinson and Governor Alexander Ramsey. War Democrats also benefited: an administration supporter, Senator Henry Rice had been a fur trader and Indian agent—indeed, the Senate nearly censured him for bilking the government on land sales. Henry Hastings Sibley, Rice's main Democratic rival, became a state militia colonel, appointed by Ramsey. But Ramsey, Rice, and Sibley had worked together before, negotiating a treaty in which Sibley claimed money meant for the Dakota, and Ramsey upheld his claim.[5]

Their choices for Bureau of Indian Affairs positions reflected the Minnesotans' political and financial interests. Wilkinson wangled the Northern Superintendency for a friend, investor Clark Thompson, giving himself control and access to money and patronage. Another loyalist, Thomas Galbraith, became the agent for the Minnesota River, where the Dakota lived; his qualification appeared to be a talent for graft.[6]

The Minnesotans took advantage of their opportunities. Saint Andre Durand Balcombe became the Winnebago agent and belied his first name, reportedly saying that he accepted such a minor post only "for the purpose of making money." Despite a corruption probe, he received $50,000 for reservation "improvements." Wilkinson told Thompson the money "will give Balcombe a chance to employ our friends this fall." Galbraith suggested that Thompson recruit officials to help defraud the government: "The *biggest* swindle please them best if they but have a *share* in" the proceeds.[7]

Efforts to combat graft there failed. In 1861 George Day became a special commissioner empowered "to use and recommend such measures as will be most likely to promote peace between the Indians and the whites." Day deemed venality the biggest obstacle to peace and sent examples to Bureau of Indian Affairs commissioner William Dole, who warned Day against sleuthing and added, "Our agents are honest & faithful." Going over Dole's head, Day apprised Lincoln, "The *whole system* is *defective* and must be revised or, your red children, as they call themselves, will *continue* to be *wronged* and outraged." Thompson responded by suggesting Day was corrupt, and Dole agreed with him. Whether Lincoln saw Day's plea is unknown, but his protests led nowhere.[8]

One problem was a change in personnel but not in approach. Through eight years of Democratic rule, Minnesota's Indians dealt with many of the same agents. Lincoln's election led to the appointment of new officials with the same corrupt outcome, but for Native Americans tragedy ensued. In 1860 Henry Whipple, the first Episcopal bishop of Minnesota, warned James Buchanan, "A nation which sowed robbery would reap a harvest of blood." Whipple proved prophetic.[9]

## The Fighting

While Lincoln spent the summer of 1862 hoping for military success, mourning his son Willie's death, and mulling emancipation, the Dakota awaited food. They finally decided to fight, against the advice of Little Crow, who warned that they were outnumbered but said, "I will die with you." On July 14 five thousand Dakota surrounded Galbraith, who described them as "getting clamorous for food." On August 2 hundreds came to the warehouse, but Galbraith doubted the situation was that dire and kept them out. When the Dakota approached with axes, an army lieutenant opened the doors to them. That helped the Dakota in the Upper Agency section. At the Lower Agency, south on the Minnesota River, where Little Crow lived, the doors stayed closed.[10]

On August 16 the payments reached the reservation, but the Dakota were unaware of that and the money produced no action. The next day four young Dakota men killed five white farm residents after they debated stealing their eggs. On August 18 several dozen Dakota came to the Lower Agency. One shot a trader who had sexually abused Dakota girls. They killed Myrick, found riddled with bullets and arrows and, honoring his suggestion, a mouthful of grass. They took as much from the stores as they and their wagons could carry and burned the buildings.

Rumors ran rampant. Reports spread quickly of five hundred white people killed and Dakota plans to attack the state capital with allies and enemies. Sibley, the militia's commander, told Ramsey that "the whole Indian force is in arms, and . . . waging a war of extermination." Unless they halted the Dakota, "the state is ruined, and some of its fairest portions will revert for years into the possession of these miserable wretches, who, among all devils in human shape, are among the most cruel and ferocious. To appreciate this, one must see, as I have, the mutilated bodies of their victims. My heart is steeled against them, and if I have the means and catch them, I will sweep them with the besom of death."[11]

Minnesota's leaders sought the means to achieve Sibley's goal. A Ramsey aide wrote to Secretary of War Edwin Stanton's deputy, "Men, women, and children are being indiscriminately murdered; evidently the result of a deep-laid plan, the attacks being simultaneous along our whole border," and requested another thousand men. Ramsey reported sending infantry to Fort Ripley amid reports that the Ojibwe (Chippewa) might attack.[12]

Minnesota Republicans begged for aid, and Lincoln's administration tried to gratify them. Ramsey asked General-in-Chief Henry Halleck to organize Minnesota into a military department with Dakota Territory under General William Harney, then in an administrative post but known as "Squaw Killer" for massacring the Lakota in the First Sioux War. Amid reports of the Union's loss at the Second Battle of Bull Run, Halleck rejected that request.[13]

Although Minnesota Republicans shared their views with Lincoln, a visitor to their state was likelier to influence him. His secretary, John Nicolay, made several troubleshooting trips. That summer Lincoln sent him to St. Paul with Dole. As talks went on with the

Ojibwe over land in northwestern Minnesota, Nicolay was to report back. Fellow secretary John Hay wrote to him, "If in the wild woods you scrounge an Indian damsel, steal her moccasins while she sleeps and bring them to me."[14]

When some Ojibwe complained about the negotiations, Nicolay's plans changed, with his party staying at Fort Ripley. Amid reports of Lee's army threatening the Capitol, Nicolay wrote to Hay, "How does your head feel? It looks very much as if it were about as safe as my scalp." He called "the mess with Hole-in-the-Day, the Chippewa chief . . . a complicated affair—involving official frauds on the one hand, and Indian depredations on the other. The Indians are in bad temper and the young braves want to fight; but they are poorly armed and have but little ammunition. . . . Hole-in-the-Day is a shrewd and intelligent and able diplomatist, and has the counsel and assistance of interested whites." On September 8 he told Hay, "We have been unable to effect any peaceable arrangement with the Chippewas. I fear they too will be in open hostility in a day or two." Two days later his group "went to Crow Wing to hold a council with the red chief. Before we knew it, he had over a hundred Indians in front of us and nearly a hundred behind us. We were surrounded. We put a bold face on the matter and went into council, spent perhaps an hour in preliminary talk after which ye gentle savage proposed to adjourn the council till next morning." In the end, state and local officials reached an agreement with the Ojibwe.[15]

With Nicolay corroborating his claims, Ramsey asked Stanton for a month's delay for Minnesota's draft and enlistment requirements. Dole said, "I have a full knowledge of all the facts, and I urge a concurrence in this request." When Stanton declined, Ramsey informed Lincoln of Dole's support and sought "an immediate answer. No one not here can conceive the panic in the state." Nicolay and Dole joined Wilkinson to add, "We are in the midst of a most terrible and exciting Indian war. Thus far the massacre of innocent white settlers has been fearful."[16]

Nicolay echoed and endorsed the Minnesotans' requests. He told Stanton that two thousand Dakota had attacked a two-hundred-mile line of settlements. White residents were "in panic and flight, leaving their harvest to waste in the field, as I have myself seen even in neighborhoods where there is no danger." Other tribes might join the attackers, he warned. "As against the Sioux, it must be a war of extermination," he said, backing Ramsey's calls for up to six thousand guns.[17]

Lincoln heeded Ramsey and Nicolay. "Attend to the Indians. If the draft cannot proceed of course it will not proceed. Necessity knows no law," he said, and he may have given Ramsey more authority than he intended by setting no deadlines. But Stanton rejected other requests, prompting Wilkinson to invite Ramsey to meet with Lincoln. Nor was Ramsey alone: Dakota Territory governor William Jayne, brother-in-law of Senator Lyman Trumbull of Illinois, feared his sparse populace might be "at the mercy of 50,000 Indians should they see proper to fall upon us" and sought additional soldiers. Iowa's Governor Samuel Kirkwood reported residents abandoning their homes, and Nebraska's territorial governor asked Stanton for "immediate action."[18]

On the day of Ramsey's request, Stanton acted on his earlier plea, telling General John Pope that he would head the Department of the Northwest: "The Indian hostilities . . . in that department," Stanton said, "require the attention of some military officer of high rank, in whose ability and vigor the government has confidence, and you have therefore been selected for this important command." He would "leave to your judgment and discretion the measures to be taken" and use "whatever force may be necessary to suppress the hostilities."[19]

Lincoln and Stanton hoped to salve Pope's wounded ego. Pope came from Illinois; Lincoln had practiced before his father, a federal judge. A West Pointer and Mexican-American War veteran, and one of Lincoln's escorts for the trip from Springfield to Washington, Pope rose through the ranks to lead the Army of the Mississippi. After victories catapulted him to major general, Lincoln called him east in the summer of 1862 to lead the new Army of Virginia. Claims like "I have come to you from the West, where we have always seen the backs of our enemies" angered his new troops. On August 29 and 30, at Second Bull Run, Robert E. Lee defeated him with a smaller army. Voicing the Union army's general attitude, one officer said, "I don't care for John Pope one pinch of owl dung"; McClellan and his allies were so slow to assist Pope's army that Republicans questioned their loyalty. Although Pope was expendable, the once-successful general and Radical Republican needed a post.[20]

Still resentful, Pope headed west. Telling Halleck that "we are likely to have a general Indian war all along the frontier, unless immediate steps are taken to put a stop to it," he added, "Unless very prompt steps are taken these states will be half depopulated before winter begins." He issued orders, sought staff, and told Sibley of plans to deploy several thousand men. He apprised Stanton, "I apprehend no further danger to the white settlements in Minnesota, but the Indians will be pursued, and, if possible, exterminated."[21]

Pope again would be disappointed. Lincoln agreed on the troops, writing, "Arm them and send them away just as fast as the Railroads will carry them." But his requests were "beyond all our expectations," Halleck said, and "cannot be filled without taking supplies from other troops now in the field. The organization of a large force for an Indian campaign is not approved by the War Department, because it is not deemed necessary." Pope complained about how few men he had to fight thousands of Dakota and repeated claims about massacres, telling Halleck about "children nailed alive to trees and houses, women violated and then disemboweled." Pope asked Stanton, "When will the paroled troops begin to arrive?" and requested more men and equipment. Halleck replied that "all that is possible will be done."[22]

However successful he was, Pope's view of Native Americans was popular in and beyond Minnesota. Pope gave Sibley an order counter to how American armies treated foreign enemies and, during the Civil War, each other: "If they desire a council, let them come in, but seize Little Crow and all others engaged in the late outrages, and hold them prisoners until further orders from these headquarters." Pope said, "It is my purpose utterly to exterminate the Sioux if I have the power to do so and even if it requires a campaign lasting the whole of next year. . . . They are to be treated as maniacs or wild beasts."[23]

Pope also wanted to show Minnesotans who was in charge. He urged Halleck to revoke Ramsey's power to raise a mounted force and eliminate trading permits among Native people. Halleck denied the first request and sent the other to the Interior Department, which ignored it. Ramsey later told Stanton that he and Pope had extended the mounted infantry to a year because, he said, "The Indian war has assumed much larger proportions than at first anticipated." Pope also sought authority to disarm the Winnebago and, when he brought up a spring offensive against Minnesota's Indians, Halleck replied, "I can no more divine than you can yourself how long you will remain in your present command," but warned "that there has been urged upon the President a proposition to remove you and appoint a civilian (a member of Congress) in your place. I need not add that I have and will oppose it."[24]

One of Pope's fellow radicals, Senator Benjamin Wade of Ohio, was behind the effort. The chair of the Joint Committee on the Conduct of the War proposed Rice, "without any disparagement of Genl. Pope, who I regard as one of our very best officers, but he has no acquaintance with the Indian character, or experience of their mode of warfare, without which, no man is competent to command against them." Wade had spent six weeks "at the head of Lake Superior," where residents feared another uprising "and have no doubt that measures should be immediately taken to prevent it. What those measures should be, Mr. Whipple will be able to inform you." Thus, Wade wanted Lincoln to consult a leading voice for reform. Forwarding Wade's letter to Stanton, Lincoln said, "I know little of Senator Rice except that he has been a very faithful friend to the Govt. in the present trouble" and suggested talking to Dole, who had just returned from Minnesota.[25]

Pope remained in command and reported success. "The Sioux war may be considered at an end," he told Halleck on October 9. Having taken 1,500 prisoners, he added, "Many are being tried by military commission for being connected with the late horrible outrages, and will be executed," suggesting the fairness of the trials. He offered to return regiments but warned of the need for a presence "along the frontier during the winter to induce settlers to return."[26]

Lincoln and some of his Cabinet had doubts. Conservative secretary of the navy Gideon Welles had no use for a radical like Pope or his report: "I was disgusted with the tone and opinions of the dispatch. It was not the production of a good man or a great one. The Indian outrages have, I doubt not, been great—what may have been the provocation we are not told. The Sioux and Ojibbeways are bad, but the Winnebages have good land which white men want and mean to have." Lincoln responded through Stanton, who said the president was considering Pope's requests and "instructs me to say" to use his men "in such manner as shall maintain the peace and secure the white inhabitants from Indian aggressions, and that upon the questions of policy presented by you his instructions will be given as soon as he shall obtain information from the Indian Department which he desires."[27]

Another issue was how to pay for Minnesota's response to the uprising. In October Ramsey assured Lincoln, "In all things I have endeavored to be economical." He added, "Our young state is feeble and poor." He suggested $150,000 would cover expenses incurred before Pope's arrival and the federal government should bear the burden. Finally, the administration and the state agreed: Stanton would ask Congress to pass a bill to compensate Minnesota.[28]

The state could make money by taking Dakota land, and Pope and the Minnesotans pursued removal. Redolent of reformers, Pope talked of the need for "education and civilization" so that "the Indians could safely be trusted among the whites." But the general also told Ramsey that Indigenous people "occupy nearly the same relation to the government as lunatics," adding, "The Sioux prisoners engaged in the late outbreak will be executed unless the President forbids it, which, from the tenor of his dispatches, I am sure he will not do."[29]

### Hanging Men for Votes?

By the time the uprising ended, the number affected was unknown. Contemporary claims of two thousand white settlers killed appear inflated. The number of Indigenous people killed remains uncertain, but of those captured by the army, 303 Dakota men went on trial. A military commission of five Minnesota officers quickly convicted them. Ramsey added, "I hope the execution of every Sioux Indian condemned by the military court will be at once ordered. It would be wrong upon principle and policy to refuse this. Private revenge would on all this border take the place of official judgment on these Indians."[30]

When Lincoln received Pope's list of those to be hanged, he made his doubts obvious. "Please forward as soon as possible the full and complete record of their convictions; and if the record does not fully indicate the more guilty and influential of the culprits, please have a careful statement made on these points and forwarded to me. Send all by mail," he wrote. Pope promised to comply but lobbied Lincoln to uphold the result. He reported that "the only distinction between the culprits is as to which of them murdered most people or violated most young girls. All of them are guilty of these things in more or less degree." Pope also warned of vigilantism: "I fear that so soon as it is known that the criminals are not at once to be executed that there will be an indiscriminate massacre of the whole. The troops are entirely new and raw, and are in full sympathy with the people on this subject. I will do the best I can, but fear a terrible result." Wilkinson, Ramsey, and Republican Representative Cyrus Aldrich chimed in to agree.[31]

Lincoln's plans prompted speculation and pressure. The views of two abolitionists suggest existing divisions. Feminist editor Jane Swisshelm, whom her friend Stanton soon hired as a War Department clerk, said, "Exterminate the wild beasts and make peace with the devil and all his hosts sooner than with these red-jawed tigers whose fangs are dripping with the blood of the innocents." By contrast, writing to *The New York Times*, abolitionist John Beeson charged that white men had provoked the Dakota and that the government had "utterly failed" to live up to its treaty obligations. Since they "are not recognized as citizens, under our Government, and not being protected by it," it would be "manifestly unjust to subject them to the penalty of laws."[32]

Lincoln's appointees felt strongly, too. Having heard from Reverend Thomas Williamson, a missionary, about the trials, Dole wrote to Smith, "I cannot reconcile it to my sense of duty to remain silent." Dole deemed the Dakota guilty of barbarity but "an indiscriminate punishment of men who have laid down their arms and surrendered themselves as prisoners, partakes more of the character of revenge than the infliction of deserved punishment . . . it is contrary to the spirit of the age, and our character as a great, magnanimous and Christian people." He doubted "beneficial results" from the hangings. Punishing "the authors of their crimes"—the "chiefs, headmen and prophets"—would do more good and avoid "a stain upon our national character, and a source of future regret." Forwarding this to Lincoln, Smith added, "Concurring in the humane views expressed by the Commissioner, I must, respectfully, ask for them your Excellency's favorable consideration."[33]

While Smith and Dole urged leniency and most Minnesotans disagreed, Lincoln heard from the public. One Minnesota doctor sent an eight-page letter "to briefly protest against the pardoning of the murderers," referring to "400 human beings, butchered, their entrails torn out, and their heads cut off and put between their lifeless thighs, or hoisted on a pole," and "a maiden of sixteen" who "had her clothes cut off in front below her breast, so as to expose her person; for three days and nights 23 painted savages satiated their lust on her, keeping her in a wood, tied to a log; she finally escaped." A missionary cited "the indignation . . . against the whole Indian people" as leading to "a great necessity . . . to execute the great majority of those who have been condemned. . . ." But he urged clemency for one Dakota he knew.[34]

A hopeful sign for the Dakota involved a proponent of executions. If asked to commute sentences, Rice told Whipple, his answer would be, "NO never!" But he had taken Whipple to meet Lincoln and promised to forward the concerns of the bishop's Episcopal colleagues to him; it was rare for them to take a political stand. Rice added, "For the honor of the government, the welfare of our frontier citizens and the good of the Indian, I most earnestly join in the prayer made to your Excellency by so many distinguished and good men" to show mercy.[35]

Amid the discussion, Lincoln sent Congress his 1862 message. It has received attention for such turns of phrase as, "Fellow-citizens, we can not escape history. . . . In giving freedom to the slave we assure freedom to the free—honorable alike in what we give and what we preserve." Although this followed a defense of delaying emancipation until 1900 and colonization, he explained, then and now, the war's meaning.[36]

But the section on the Dakota lacked this sensitivity. He began, "The Indian tribes upon our frontiers have during the past year manifested a spirit of insubordination, and at several points have engaged in open hostilities against the white settlements in their vicinity." The Dakota had acted "with extreme ferocity, killing, indiscriminately, men, women, and children. This attack was wholly unexpected, and, therefore, no means of defence had been provided," which took Pope and Minnesota Republicans at face value. Reporting an estimated eight hundred deaths and property damage, he wrote, "How this outbreak was induced is not definitely known, and suspicions, which may be unjust, need not to be stated." But Dole's Bureau had heard of plans for "a simultaneous attack . . . upon the white settlements by all the tribes between the Mississippi river and the Rocky mountains." By suggesting outside influences, Lincoln painted the Dakota as victims or accomplices of wily enemies.[37]

Lincoln's solution proved consistent with his ideology and history. Minnesotans "manifest much anxiety for the removal of the tribes beyond the limits of the State as a guarantee against future hostilities," he wrote, leaving details to Dole. Indian removal already was common, and he supported colonizing African Americans, although that would be voluntary while the Dakota would have to leave Minnesota. In keeping with his antislavery views, and Whipple's pleas, he sought reforms. But his next lines hailed progress on the Pacific railroad, which required keeping Native people out of its way, by force if necessary.[38]

On the day of his message, Lincoln turned to the trials. "I wish your legal opinion whether if I should conclude to execute only a part of them, I must myself designate which," he wrote to Judge Advocate General Joseph Holt. He replied that only Lincoln could decide. Lincoln then asked three Interior Department officials—Smith's deputy John Usher, clerk George Whiting, and lawyer Francis Ruggles—to search the material for particular acts: rape and killing women and children. They found some trials that took just a few minutes, which attorneys like Lincoln were likely to find dubious.[39]

Clearly, Lincoln saw executing 303 Dakota as excessive. The Cabinet met on December 4. Welles wrote, "The Members of Congress from Minnesota are urging the President vehemently to give his assent to the execution of the three hundred Indian captives, but they will not succeed." But Welles had no sympathy for Native Americans: "When the intelligent Representatives of a State can deliberately besiege the Government to take the lives of these ignorant barbarians by wholesale, after they have surrendered themselves prisoners, it would [seem] the sentiments of the Representatives were but slightly removed from the barbarians whom they would execute."[40]

Two days later Lincoln announced his decision. Interior personnel listed the thirty-nine who met his standard for execution (he commuted another later). Writing out the names in a dispatch to Sibley, he added, "The other condemned prisoners you will hold subject to further orders, taking care that they neither escape, nor are subjected to any unlawful violence," suggesting his feelings about vigilante justice. He told Nicolay to copy it and send it to Sibley via a special messenger.[41]

Wilkinson's update to Ramsey on Lincoln's decision struck several unusual notes. On December 9 Wilkinson said, "I have done all in my power to induce our President to have the law executed in regard to your condemned Indians"; now they were "your" Dakota. Convinced, as many were, that they could persuade or bully Lincoln, Wilkinson said, "We have made some impression upon him, and he has at last consented to order the execution of 39, but he will not permit the others to be discharged, but will order them held for the present." Wilkinson counseled waiting: "If the people will be patient we will be able, I think, to dispose of those condemned, and will also succeed in removing the Sioux and Winnebago Indians from the state."[42]

Lincoln gave further details in response to a Senate resolution. On December 5 the Senate asked for "all information in his possession touching the late Indian barbarities in the State of Minnesota and also the evidence in his possession upon which some of the principal actors and head men were tried and condemned to death." Lincoln sent Dole's answer six days later with a letter from Minnesota officials that "contains some statements of fact not found in the records of the trial." He chose not to send "appeals in behalf of the condemned, appeals for their execution, and expressions of opinion as to proper policy in regard to them, and to the Indians generally in that vicinity, none of which, as I understand, falls within the scope of your inquiry."[43]

Lincoln made clear that threats and demands had no effect. "Anxious to not act with so much clemency as to encourage another outbreak on the one hand, nor with so much severity as to be real cruelty on the other," he said, "I caused a careful examination of the records of trials to be made, in view of first ordering the execution of such as had been proved guilty of violating females. Contrary to my expectations, only two of this class were found," which rebuked officials accusing the Dakota of indiscriminate rapes. Lincoln then checked for those "proven to have participated in massacres" and not battles, and found thirty-eight more. At the request of those who tried the cases, he commuted the sentence for one person who provided information on the others. "In a finish that is pure Lincoln," as one scholar said, Lincoln wrote the list of names, many of them long, by hand and spelled them phonetically to make sure the executioner made no mistakes.[44]

Whether Lincoln hoped to put this behind him or deemed it inhumane or impolitic to wait too long, he informed the Senate the executions would take place on December 19. But the Minnesotans wanted more time. Sibley replied, "They are imprisoned at Mankato 90 miles distant and the time fixed . . . is too short for preparation and for concentrating the troops necessary to protect the other Indians and preserve the peace. The excitement prevails [in] all sections of the state and secret combinations exist embracing thousands of citizens pledged to execute all the Indians." On December 16 Lincoln wrote to Sibley, "As you suggest, let the execution fixed for Friday, the 19th instant, be postponed to, and be done on, Friday, the 26th instant."[45]

*The New York Times* editorialized on the subject and, as usual, editor Henry Raymond followed Lincoln. "From the statements at first made in regard to these Indian troubles in Minnesota, we favored a policy of even greater clemency than the President has adopted," the *Times* said, "but the evidence since published, reveals atrocities on the part of the savages so inexcusable, cold-blooded and shocking, that we cannot differ from the decision the President has made after his perusal of that evidence." The *Times* also suggested that with Minnesota Native people "so thoroughly scared at the fury of the whites," the administration "should take them under its supervision and transport the whole body of them out of the State—say down to Indian Territory."[46]

On December 27 came Sibley's update: "I have the honor to inform you that the 38 Indians and half-breeds ordered by you for execution were hung yesterday at Mankato, at 10 a.m. Everything went off quietly." With about a thousand troops guarding the area, the thirty-eight went to the gallows singing Dakota death songs and held hands as the executioners put white muslin over their heads and ropes around their necks. The hangings prompted "one, not loud, but prolonged cheer from the soldiery and citizens who were spectators, and then all were quiet and earnest witnesses of the scene." One company interred them in two rows. Those who received commutations "were much dejected all day," a reporter wrote. So were Minnesotans who wanted more executions. After the 1864 election, when Ramsey told him that his majority in Minnesota would have been larger without so many commutations, Lincoln replied, "I could not afford to hang men for votes."[47]

## Meanings

The executions were not an ending, but the beginning of a discussion without end. In 1863, convinced of the Dakota threat, Pope launched an offensive into Dakota Territory. After Congress ignored warnings about the area, Dole reported, those who fled to Dakota did "all in their power, and it would appear with success, to induce their brethren to make common cause with them in an endeavor to exterminate and drive all whites from the Territory." Pope wanted his men to follow the Indians into Canada; Halleck had to remind him that was British territory and a matter for the president to decide. Pope tried to wrest control of Indian policy from the Interior Department back to the War Department by criticizing treaties and annuities as breeding corruption, and proposing trade policies to improve how Native people and the government dealt with one another. Thus Pope simultaneously pursued extermination and reform, much as the United States did for decades.[48]

Lincoln and his administration mistreated the Dakota, and later let Minnesotans pursue them beyond state lines, but also sought some degree of fairness—as they defined it. In 1864 Williamson asked Lincoln to pardon those held at Camp McClellan in Iowa. Dole advised Lincoln, "I do not believe any injury will accrue to the white people if you should exercise the pardoning power in favour of a portion of these people and I have so much confidence in . . . Mr. Williamson that I have no hesitancy in uniting in his recommendation in favor of the particular persons named by him." Lincoln then ordered the pardons.[49]

Rumors still churned that outside sources had played a role in causing the uprising. *The New York Times* heard "from a gentleman whose statements and proofs seem to be beyond dispute" that rebels had plotted the uprising as "part of a grand scheme of frontier butcheries." In an editorial beside its republication of Lincoln's letter responding to editor Horace Greeley's call for emancipation in his earlier editorial "The Prayer of 20 Millions," the *New York Tribune* declared, "The Sioux have doubtless been stimulated if not bribed to plunder and slaughter their White neighbors by White and Red villains sent among them for this purpose by the Secessionists" (little did Greeley know that after a loss, Little Crow had said, "It must be the work of traitors in our midst" since "we are brave men, while they are cowardly women"). From Canada, where he was consul general, abolitionist Joshua Giddings had "little doubt" that "secession agents, operating through Canadian Indians and fur traders," had egged on the Ojibwe. Beeson said this ignored the fact that Native Americans considered themselves "a sovereign people," and "their hostile acts in Minnesota as one of war, and not rebellion; and for what the most civilized nations would deem sufficient occasion for war." In December 1862 Smith saw "the chief cause . . . in the insurrection of the southern states," which may have been true given the funds and manpower directed elsewhere. But in March, when Lincoln sent the final report on Minnesota to the House, Usher, Smith's successor, admitted that "the real cause of outbreak is difficult, if not impossible, to determine."[50]

In months to come, Lincoln and Congress resolved where the Dakota would live. Days after the commutations, Wilkinson and William Windom, a congressman from Minnesota, introduced a bill to banish the Dakota and Winnebago, possibly with administration support. State officials wanted them gone, and federal officials may have wanted to appease them. Dole viewed the Winnebago as no more responsible for the uprising than "our government would be for [the acts] of a pirate who might happen to have been born upon our territory." In March 1863 Congress approved their removal, and the administration agreed.[51]

In May federal officials led about 1,300 Dakota, mostly women and children, to two steamers headed for the Upper Missouri River. Some Minnesotans threw rocks at their boat, but others just welcomed the chance to take their land. Those sent to Dakota Territory, where most of the men had joined Little Crow, faced a drought, but the Bureau of Indian Affairs lacked funds to help. Making matters worse, the Dakota had a poor relationship with the Winnebago relocated with them.[52]

Nor was the administration honest about the situation. In 1863 Dole's annual report described their two reservations, "in point of fertility, healthful climate, excellence of timber and water, and in all the necessary requirements for a thriving and happy community," as "unsurpassed by any within our borders." He said that "ample provisions had been made for their physical, intellectual, and moral cultivation, and no doubt could be entertained that the patient and persevering efforts which were being made for their improvement and happiness would . . . finally result in complete success. Now all is changed." So it was, but no Dakota would have recognized the Edenic world that Dole described.[53]

What the Dakota uprising and its results mean for our view of Lincoln is debatable. He approved the biggest mass execution in American history and removed Native peoples from their land. Compared with how his view of African Americans evolved, Indigenous people fared much worse. Despite politics, Lincoln spared lives that might have been lost under another president; few other nineteenth-century presidents would have been likely to show his restraint, granting that he could have been even more restrained.[54]

The trials of the Dakota also had a deeper legal meaning. As John Fabian Witt wrote in his study of the administration's code of war, "the more interesting question is not whether the military commission trials were paragons of civil libertarian virtue (they were not), or even whether they lived up to the already dubious standards of trials in nineteenth-century courts (they did not). The real question is why U.S. officials held trials at all," because summary executions of Native Americans were nothing new. Sibley in particular may have seen this as another step in defeating the Dakota because further attacks on them were difficult, given such factors as manpower and weather. But the next year, political scientist Francis Lieber wrote a wartime legal code at the War Department's request. Lieber already had advised his old friend Halleck on legal matters and had no issue with excepting Native Americans from some of his provisions—but he also disclaimed torture as a punishment, asking, "Can we roast Indians though they may have roasted one of our own," and concluding, as several of Lincoln's advisers on the Dakota trials did, they could not.[55]

Critically, though, Lieber's "Code of War," issued in 1863 as General Orders No. 100, came after the Dakota uprising and trials. How much they influenced what he wrote and why Lincoln's administration asked him to write it are uncertain. But the use of a military trial at a time when it was less common (even if only as an extension of military action), especially for Native Americans, and Lincoln's desire for some kind of fairness suggested a degree of respect for law not seen in previous administrations, and a potential effect of the Dakota uprising.

The uprising may have shaped other policies. On August 23 Lincoln opposed enlisting African American soldiers, but two days later he changed his mind. Perhaps he was cautious, as his reply to Greeley's "prayer" for emancipation suggests. That day, however, he received Ramsey's request to delay the draft in Minnesota and warnings from Nebraska Territory of a Native uprising. Together, they could have had an impact. Scott Berg also made a telling point in his account of the Dakota uprising: "Operating during a slice of time when white warfare hung between ages-old chivalric ideals and the brutal realities of 'total war,' the Dakota had killed 93 white soldiers and between 400 and 600 white civilians," many of them not directly involved in mistreating the Dakota. Two years later a Union general took the position that civilians had to feel the effects of war and accordingly cut a swath through the South. His middle name was Tecumseh.[56]

## PEOPLING AND UNPEOPLING
## THE WEST

On April 14, 1865, Abraham Lincoln met with Schuyler Colfax for the last time and managed to capture the Republican ideology of free labor and its application to Native Americans. The Speaker of the House planned a trip to California with *Springfield Republican* editor Samuel Bowles. "I have very large ideas of the mineral wealth of our nation. I believe it practically inexhaustible. It abounds all over the western country, from the Rocky Mountains to the Pacific, and its development has scarcely commenced," Lincoln said. Although he believed western mines could ease the Union's debt, "I did not care about encouraging the increase in the volume of our precious metals. We had the country to save first." As it turned out, the mining rushes attracted enough interest without his encouragement.[1]

Lincoln's plans typified his party's wartime and postwar goals. "We shall have hundreds of thousands of disbanded soldiers, and many have feared that their return home in such great numbers might paralyze industry by furnishing suddenly a greater supply of labor than there will be a demand for. I am going to try and attract them to the hidden wealth of our mountain ranges, where there is room enough for all," he said. As European immigrants arrived, "I intend to point them to the gold and silver that waits for them in the West. Tell the miners from me that I shall promote their interests to the utmost of my ability, because their prosperity is the prosperity of the nation; and we shall prove, in a very few years, that we are, indeed, the *treasury of the world*" while peopling recently acquired land. As in settler colonialism, the conqueror sought to eliminate all vestiges of the conquered; in keeping with the free labor ideology, Lincoln wanted the land for Anglos.[2]

Republicans first united to keep slavery out of western territories and spread free labor, which mining and agriculture would make the center of the western economy. Lincoln and his party did their best (and worst) to aid western interests, passing legislation and promoting migration and moneymaking while the government exerted its power, all to the detriment of Indigenous people. Lincoln's second interior secretary, John Usher, said, "This Department will make provision for such Indians as will submit to its authority and locate upon the reservation. Those who resist should be pursued by the military, and punished." They meant to control Native Americans in ways consistent with the past and foreshadowing the future: moving them where whites wanted them to be, through reservations and concentration.[3]

Forcing large numbers of people to move was nothing new. Lincoln still pondered Black colonization. In August 1863, believing they encouraged rebel raids, General Thomas Ewing Jr. ordered Anglo residents out of four Missouri counties along the Kansas line. While the Trail of Tears was the most tragic example, Indian removal long had been federal policy. Now Lincoln hoped to populate, improve, and protect a continental empire. Intended or not, Native Americans would suffer for it in similar ways throughout the West, but with key differences depending on geography and Native-white relations.[4]

### Lincoln and His Party Look West

The combination of Lincoln's victory in 1860 and secession enabled Republicans to enact their agenda for the West and heightened the West's importance. Fighting to protect slavery, the South hoped to add the West to a slaveholding empire. With the Union hoping to retain the West, Republicans dreaming of populating the area with free laborers, the South out of the Union, and Democrats in the minority, Lincoln and his allies welcomed the power and opportunity to act.[5]

Three bills in 1862 especially shaped the West and involved land won or taken from Native Americans. To fund colleges for training in technology and agriculture, the Morrill Act used money from the sales of public lands. Republicans hoped the Homestead Act would help thousands of families migrate west and farm. The Pacific Railroad Act set up a transcontinental line, with the privately owned, government-subsidized Central Pacific going east from Sacramento and the Union Pacific driving west from Omaha as a private-public partnership. Both prompted graft and unprecedented federal investment in a public works project that crossed the West and warmed the hearts of ex-Whigs like Lincoln. Two years later his annual message referred to the West and the need "to render it secure for the advancing settler," which meshed with policies toward its Indigenous people. Lincoln said little about these issues, but just as politicians he worked with and generals he chose battled the Confederacy to the east, his appointees proved crucial in the far West. They sought to clear the way for the mining and railroads he saw as inseparable from the nation's growth.[6]

Seeking to people the West, Republicans resurrected a historical contradiction. Edmund Morgan described the "paradox" of colonial Virginians spreading slavery in the service of freedom: slave labor gave them the wealth and education to build a country. Hoping to limit where slavery could grow, many Republicans claimed to act in Native Americans' best interests by forcing them onto reservations—much as those who enslaved Africans claimed to rescue them from benighted status. It reeked of settler colonialism, and Lincoln and Republicans created their version of the paradox: historian Durwood Ball wrote, "Union volunteers simply had to deprive Native Americans of their freedom to advance their own liberty in the American West."[7]

### California and Genocide

The administration wanted safe passage for travelers and railroad construction, but California's potential as an entrepôt for Asian markets, and its fields of gold and crops, won it special attention. California Indians suffered a genocide, their population falling from 150,000 in 1846 to 30,000 by 1870. When Lincoln took office, the die had long since been cast. During his tenure the army attacked Native Americans, while his appointees cost more lives by trying to concentrate them.[8]

At the Bureau of Indian Affairs, William Dole deemed California a laboratory for reform. In 1861, referring to mass murders in northern counties, he said, "The Indians are hunted like wild and dangerous beasts of prey; the parents are 'murdered,' and the children 'kidnapped.'" He accused whites of "the perversion of power and of cruel wrong, from which humanity instinctively recoils." Dole proposed eliminating one of the state's two superintendents and combining Indigenous Californians onto four reservations. To avoid appointees susceptible to corruption, he named a special agent "to report upon measures of reform" and "clothed with necessary powers to prevent all such collisions between the Indians and the whites as are avoidable."[9]

Other leaders agreed. Senate Indian Committee chair James Doolittle of Wisconsin lamented that California's tribes "have been fading away as the white population has been advancing on them." He empathized with their plight: "Their game, their means of living, being destroyed, they are reduced to that condition where from the very necessities of their position they are sometimes tempted to plunder upon the white population, to steal, in order to live, rather than starve." His committee backed Dole's actions, but California's congressional delegation fought the legislation and headed off most of the changes.[10]

As Republicans pursued concentration, other problems plagued California's Native Americans. Drought struck their reservations. Long-standing local support for kidnapping and enslaving them continued. Food rations dropped precipitously. Fighting continued in northern counties, with the Hoopa gaining better reservation land in a peace treaty and the Modoc surrendering and forced to go to Oregon.[11]

To the south, genocide proved an apt description. Responding to incursions, Owens River Valley Indians stole livestock from ranches near Santa Barbara and Los Angeles. In January 1865, in the Owens Valley War, settlers killed most residents of one village and forced dozens more Indians into Owens Lake and massacred them. Reform and concentration required public support; Californians showed no such inclinations, nor were Lincoln and his aides willing or able to overcome them.[12]

## The Greater Basin

For Lincoln and his party, issues in the Great Basin went beyond Native American policies to deal with distinct Anglo cultures. After arriving in 1847, Mormons dominated what became Utah Territory. In 1857 the army marched there amid claims of Mormon rebellion against federal rule. Cooler heads prevailed, but the army stayed in Utah until the Civil War began. Turnover among federal officials did nothing to ease tensions: In four years, five superintendents held Utah's Indian affairs slot. In three years, Lincoln named three governors, all Indiana politicians. John Dawson left, claiming Mormon vigilantes assaulted him; Stephen Harding warned constantly of an imminent Mormon uprising. Finally, Lincoln turned to James Doty.[13]

Doty's promotion followed a term as Utah's Indian superintendent, where he combined the negotiation and violence typical of Native-white relations—as historian Ned Blackhawk put it, "massacre and peace interwoven." The pending railroad and protecting routes for ore and mail were a priority for federal officials, many of whom believed that Mormons helped Native Americans prey on travelers and the military. Doty pursued the policy as superintendent that Usher later described: separating and controlling Native Americans in one place.[14]

Doty did rely on negotiation. In 1861 Lincoln approved two million acres of the lush Uintah Valley, far from travel routes, for a reservation. But, lacking supplies and land, Native peoples still conducted raids. Doty met with them, the *New York Tribune* said, hoping to "restrain them from further outrages. Their lands do not furnish sufficient hunting and fishing to support them, and it is feared that the former Superintendent withheld supplies due from Government, so that they have been driven by necessity to plunder emigrant trains." The *Tribune* claimed Mormons "inflamed [Indians'] minds against the Government. . . . Troops may be required to take care of the Mormons."[15]

New soldiers arriving in late 1862 created new issues. Californians under Colonel Patrick Connor came to protect travel routes, especially from the Shoshone (Newe), who resented encroachments and loss of supplies. Native-white relations in Utah "are still in an unsatisfactory condition. But little progress has been made in sub-jecting the Indians to the policy we have adopted for their govern-ment," Dole said, and he echoed that the next year. Territorial officials blamed the Shoshone and Snake for most of the raids. In turn, Con-nor attacked Native settlements, exerting power that helped Doty's treaty-making.[16]

Unfortunately, one of Connor's excursions typified the army's ap-proach to Native peoples, especially in the West. The Newe camped at Bear River in present-day Idaho. Press reports claimed they vowed to kill every white man they met. Accusing them of murdering mi-grants to Montana and Washington Territories, Connor decided "to chastise them, if possible." He and his infantry and cavalry went north in January 1863 and found them entrenched. On January 29, in a four-hour fight known as the Bear River Massacre, about two dozen Union soldiers died; estimates of Newe deaths ranged from 250 to 400. Connor later declared, "It was not my intention to take any prisoners."[17]

News coverage both reflected and questioned his views. The *Deseret News*, the voice of the church that Connor disdained, said that "with ordinary good luck, the volunteers will 'wipe them out.' We wish this community rid of all such parties, and if Col. Connor be successful in reaching that bastard class of humans who play with the lives of the peaceable and law-abiding citizens in this way, we shall be pleased to acknowledge our obligations." Connor could say, "'I went, I fought, I conquered, I exterminated,'" wrote a *New York Times* reporter, but amid rumors of more Dakota unrest, he asked: If events in Minnesota "result in a general Indian ugliness in the North, will the Connor expedition not still further incense the Indians left?" The *New York Tribune* was less concerned: "These Indians had murdered several miners during the winter, and were a part of the same band who had been massacring emigrants."[18]

What Lincoln thought is unknown, but Mormons and travelers welcomed the results. The Western Shoshone largely ceased to be a threat. Mormons extended their networks farther from Salt Lake. Traveling to and from western mines became safer. According to the

*Times*'s Salt Lake correspondent, "for his great victory" Connor won a promotion to brigadier general, approved by the War Department. By then Lincoln had signed the Pacific Railway Act and could ill afford to ignore concerns about travel routes. Further, Lincoln had just faced political fire for pardoning Dakota in Minnesota. Bear River was farther away, with neither influential figures nor electoral votes to worry about. If he knew about Bear River, it may not have mattered.[19]

Nevada Territory, in the western Great Basin, posed similar problems but prompted different solutions. The Comstock mining rush drove a population boom, and settlers and Northern Paiutes fought in 1860. No comparable violence recurred, but federal officials feared what *The New York Times* reported two years later: "All the white folks are deserting the Northern routes . . . as life and property are now so very uncertain." The Newe attacked travelers, and soldiers headed for Utah under Connor and Arizona under James Carleton. Nevada governor James Nye, once a cog in New York's political machine, had limited experience with Indigenous people, but his choice as agent, Warren Wasson, was a Bureau veteran. They visited tribes, bringing food and, in keeping with policy, urging them to farm.[20]

The federal presence and threats heightened tensions amid the combination of negotiation and attack. Late in 1861, with Nye upset over raids and a "troublesome" chief, Wasson went to central Nevada and negotiated a treaty acknowledging Newe land ownership and easing tensions, but it went unratified. In 1862, after the army set up a fort in Ruby Valley, Connor recruited Newe as scouts and informants but ordered that if "friendly Indians deliver to you Indians who were concerned in the late murder of emigrants, you will (being satisfied of their guilt) immediately hang them, and leave their bodies thus exposed as an example of what evildoers may expect."[21]

With Lincoln signing the Pacific Railroad Act, and construction to begin on the transcontinental line, federal control grew even more important. Nye and Doty converged on Ruby Valley near the Nevada-Utah line and agreed to a treaty of "Peace and Friendship" on October 1, 1863. The federal government could build forts and postal stations and would provide $5,000 annually to the Newe, who agreed to be peaceful. Whites could dig for ore and settle on their land. Only if the president "shall deem it expedient for them to abandon the roaming life . . . and become herdsmen or agriculturalists" would they have to move to reservations. A few days later, the Shoshone-Goship Treaty contained similar provisions for western Utah Territory.[22]

Whether Lincoln read the treaties is doubtful, but his appointees were pleased. A year later, Nye said the Newe "have been quiet and have conducted themselves peaceably and commendably." But the negotiations represented only about one-quarter of those identified, on their own or by the Bureau, as Newe. Despite provisions acknowledging Native ownership, white settlers claimed the land, and the Newe wound up without their land or the money they deserved for it.[23]

The treaties also fit into a broader policy of improving, denigrating, and removing Native Americans. Nye expected them to "be educated in all the useful branches of common education and ordinary agriculture, [which would] transform them from savages to men and women adapted to all the employments necessary to self-subsistence," and cheered "that a nation, while struggling for its existence against a mighty rebellion, with one hand . . . stretches out the other with kindness over the long-neglected savage for his redemption." Meanwhile the army commander in the vicinity committed a massacre at Bear River. The federal government sought to reduce Native influence and used varied means to do so. The Great Basin demonstrated their interplay.[24]

### Sand Creek

Events at Sand Creek represented a bloodier, more radical version of developments elsewhere in the West. Politics, economics, growth, and prevailing attitudes affected Indians everywhere but were writ large in Colorado Territory. Yet just as the war hastened emancipation, the Sand Creek Massacre prompted reforms in Indian policy, though after Lincoln had died. Unfortunately, the immediate benefits of these changes lacked the long-term impact they should have had.[25]

As in Nevada Territory, created along with Colorado in 1861, mines and those traveling to them prompted white encroachment on Native land to a degree far greater than at any previous time. When questions over reservations and trade left unclear boundaries, settlers moved into disputed areas anyway. After Dole ruled that the federal government still had jurisdiction over profitable mining and farm land as well as the nascent town of Denver, territorial leaders complained. Dole backed down, and Colorado again was wide open.[26]

Lincoln's territorial governors made a bad situation worse. Like many appointees, William Gilpin in Colorado owed his job to a key ally: fellow Missourian Frank Blair, whose family included some of Lincoln's closest advisers. Gilpin fretted about battling Native Americans or that they would prey on travelers. He wound up facing corruption charges until Lincoln removed him in 1862. His successor, Illinois investor John Evans, already had rejected an offer to govern Washington Territory but saw political and economic opportunity in Colorado.[27]

Just as settlement in Colorado imperiled Native Americans, so did political and governmental ambitions. Evans lobbied for Union Pacific construction through the territory and hoped to keep Native people from interfering. He also joined a drive for statehood. Nicolay described the area as "already a civilized country . . . a land of active enterprise, where all classes of people are prosperous." Nonetheless, Colorado residents doubted "active enterprise" could continue without a state government to exert control and elected federal congressmen to represent their interests, which included controlling Native people.[28]

Evans pursued the administration's policy of concentration. The Treaty of Fort Wise in 1861 moved more Colorado Natives onto a reservation, but not all Cheyenne and Arapaho accepted it. After Dole told Evans to work with New Mexico officials to shift all Utes onto reservations, the ensuing meeting produced a treaty that Evans called "one of the most extensive and perhaps the most valuable cessions ever secured in a single treaty from any tribe of Indians in the country." In reality, Colorado's Indigenous people remained unconcentrated.[29]

In 1864 several factors heightened tension there. As was the case elsewhere, a reduced food supply forced Indians to conduct raids, prompting Evans to warn of "several thousand warriors" allied "for the purpose of waging war." He added, "A peace before conquest, in this case would be the most *cruel* kindness and the most *barbarous* humanity." That June, Indians killed the Hungate family (a rancher and his wife and two daughters) near Denver, and local authorities increased agitation by displaying their remains publicly.[30]

Evans and his commander, Colonel John Chivington, capitalized on these fears and provocations. Calling on "friendly Indians" to unite with "the Great Father," Evans urged Coloradans "to go in pursuit of all hostile Indians on the plains" and obtained War Department aid. The new Third Colorado, given one hundred days to serve under Chivington, was to "pursue, kill, and destroy all hostile Indians that infest the plains, for thus only can we secure a permanent and lasting peace." Chivington hoped military glory might boost his political fortunes, and he joined Evans to meet with Black Kettle and other Cheyenne and Arapaho leaders. They denied Black Kettle's request to go to nearby Fort Lyon; according to Chivington, the tribes reneged on promises to return hostages and stolen animals, and he removed that fort's commander for promising safe lodging. Forced to go to Big Sandy Creek, an Arkansas River tributary, Black Kettle's Cheyenne and Chief Niwot's Arapaho flew an American flag and a white flag to signify their peaceful intent, but whites suspected different motives.[31]

After the Hungate deaths, General Samuel Curtis, the area's overall commander, told Chivington to "crush the Indians." Ignoring other Natives who had actually resisted white incursions, Chivington led more than 250 men, almost done with their enlistments, toward Sand Creek (as the area by Big Sandy Creek was known). On the morning of November 29, they attacked. By Chivington's exaggerated count, they killed five hundred Natives. Not only did they murder unarmed Cheyenne and Arapaho; soldiers massacred women and children, cut off fingers for souvenirs, and scalped and sexually mutilated their victims.[32]

While the settlers won the battle for the land, Evans and Chivington lost the war for public opinion. As one commander said, Chivington "whipped the only peaceable Indians in the country." No longer peaceable, Cheyenne and Arapaho conducted raids and attacked soldiers. The massacre gutted the Coloradans' political ambitions, with Evans forced to resign and Chivington never holding a major office.[33]

Demonstrating contempt for Native Americans and the truth, Chivington tried to capitalize on his version of events. He "used the gallons of blood spilled along Sand Creek to depict a masterstroke," Ari Kelman has written in his study of the massacre and its meaning. Claiming proof of scalping, Chivington wrote, "The evidence is most conclusive that these Indians are the worst that have infested the routes on the Platte and Arkansas Rivers." He described fighting "one of the most powerful villages of the Cheyenne Nation" and "almost an entire annihilation of the entire tribe."[34]

Ensuing investigations produced a different, more truthful narrative. After ranking Chivington's victory "among the brilliant feats of arms in Indian warfare," the *Rocky Mountain News* reported a congressional probe: "Letters received from high officials in Colorado say that the Indians were killed after surrendering, and that a large proportion of them were women and children"; the high official was the territorial chief justice, another Lincoln appointee. The army sent Patrick Wynkoop, whom Chivington had relieved at Fort Lyon for being too sympathetic toward the Cheyenne, to look into the matter; his report called Chivington an "inhuman monster." The War Department and the Joint Congressional Committee on the Conduct of the War conducted in-depth studies, and news accounts began to spread of what had happened.[35]

Joint Committee chair Ben Wade's summary was withering. Evans engaged in "such prevarication and shuffling as has been shown by no witness" in the committee's four years of hearings. Evans refused to admit that the victims had "the most friendly feelings towards the whites, and had done all in their power to restrain those less friendly disposed"; none of those "guilty of acts of hostility" had been with Black Kettle. The Radical Republican senator from Ohio said, "What Indians he would ever term friendly it is impossible to tell." Assailing Chivington's "mission of murder and barbarity," the committee accused him of shrinking from attacking the legitimately hostile. Wade hoped for punishment for those who had committed "these brutal and cowardly acts," and policies to end "the employment of officers, civil and military, such as have heretofore made the administration of Indian affairs in this country a byword and reproach." Wade said all of the right things without suggesting that the problems predated Sand Creek.[36]

Politically, the massacre and investigations had important effects. Soon after taking office, Andrew Johnson's administration asked Evans to resign, exacerbating a divide over statehood and contributing to a "Sand Creek Vindication" effort. Evans's successor, Alexander Cummings, reported, "There is no place for any United States officer here unless he will endorse all the horrible atrocities of Sand Creek and utterly ignore the famous frauds in the Quartermaster Department by which the government was swindled out of millions of dollars under pretence of suppressing Indian hostilities." As the railroad, settlers, and the army swept through the West, atrocities, fraud, and feelings about Sand Creek, whether justification or atonement, mattered less than controlling the land—the quest that drove the massacre.[37]

But Sand Creek did prompt some change. Congress provided the Cheyenne and Arapaho what historian David Nichols called $40,000 in "conscience money." Doolittle said reports of the massacre could "make one's blood chill and freeze with horror" and urged reforms. The popular view of Native peoples as savages suffered, if briefly, with the realization that white peoples could be worse. And the investigations pointed in directions that reformers urged upon Lincoln. In 1867 a joint congressional committee reported on the need for different federal policies; two years later new president Ulysses Grant heeded them with his "peace policy," which involved church groups in administering Native affairs. The committee also directed blame where it belonged: at those encroaching on traditional Indian land.[38]

Lincoln's response can only be conjectured. A Dole critic suggested Lincoln contemplated ousting him after Sand Creek, but the outcry began amid Lincoln's push for the Thirteenth Amendment, followed by the war's end and his assassination. What he thought of Sand Creek is unknown; he might have deferred to Congress, from constitutional scruples and because he knew the will for reform required others to act. When he told Wilkinson, referring to the Dakota, "I could not hang men for votes," he distinguished himself from Colorado's leaders. But he put them, or those who chose them, in their posts.[39]

## The Long Walk

Whatever Lincoln's intentions, his policies had a sad symmetry. As the Civil War began, Winfield Scott had been general-in-chief since 1841 when he oversaw the Trail of Tears, for which Lincoln had lauded him. Later in the war James Carleton, one of Scott's soldiers in the Mexican-American War, forced the Navajo (Diné) into their version of the Trail of Tears. The government drove tribes from the South so as to open land to agriculture and slavery, and it acted similarly under Lincoln in the West: "to foster and protect our own settlements, to secure the ultimate perpetuity of the Territory, and a speedy development of its resources, and to reclaim and civilize the Indians," as Dole said—in that order.[40]

The process proved both easier and harder than Dole may have expected. The Confederacy had designs on the Southwest, which attracted Jefferson Davis's attention when he was secretary of war (1853–57). The three-day Battle of Glorieta Pass, east of Santa Fe in 1862, was called "the Gettysburg of the West," though less bloody or storied. It largely ended rebel hopes of westward growth, just as Gettysburg and Vicksburg sealed the South's fate. Although Union officials still stressed the need to protect the West and its goldfields from the South, they turned increasingly to what they saw as an internal threat: Native Americans.[41]

Splitting New Mexico by creating Arizona Territory in 1863 changed boundaries but not the views of federal officials, who sought to stop Indians and Mexicans from livestock raids and trading captives with one another. They hoped moving Natives to reservations—one for the Apache and one for the Diné—would break that cycle and protect gold seekers. As New Mexico's superintendant of Indian affairs said, "No civil authority can be exercised over these hostile tribes and bands until they are thoroughly convinced of the power of the government."[42]

Which tribes and bands were hostile should have mattered more to federal officials but did not. Early in Lincoln's tenure, the area's Indians—especially along the New Mexico-Colorado line—complained about encroachments by miners. New Mexico superintendent James Collins tried to help, including urging the government to indemnify Utes for lost hunting land. The Senate refused, so Utes conducted raids—especially late in 1862 when the Bureau provided too little food. The army helped with food sent by order of its commander, Carleton.[43]

Thus the irony of Carleton's destructive policies. An agent reported "a continuous state of hostility" among Mescalero Apache that endangered Arizona's mining industry. Although Apache leader Mangas Coloradas was "anxious for peace" and said that Americans "attacked & killed many of his people," Carleton ordered his lieutenant, Indian fighter and scout Kit Carson, to end Apache resistance: "All Indian men of that tribe are to be killed whenever and wherever you can find them." By early 1863 Carson's attacks had subdued them.[44]

The desire to control Native Americans and protect mining prompted Bosque Redondo, Carleton's effort to concentrate the Diné. The Apache response to white settlers paled in comparison to the Diné, who faced charges of filching three hundred horses and cattle and ten thousand sheep in less than a month. Although few Navajo were involved, early in 1863 Carleton presented his terms: surrender within three months and relocate to a reservation in eastern New Mexico, or Carson would attack. That July, claiming, "Entire subjugation, or destruction of all the men, are the alternatives," Carleton ordered him into action.[45]

The results met Carleton's hopes. Working with tribal foes of the Diné, Carson destroyed their crops and took their livestock. *The New York Times* cheered, "That fierce and untameable tribe of redskins . . . are reported to have lately surrendered to our forces in New-Mexico." Noting the administration sought $100,000 from Congress, the *Times* doubted "that it will be more economical to support the Navajoes than to fight them . . . though on grounds of humanity, we might concede the wisdom of giving these galloping wretches rations of bread and beef rather than of bullets and cold steel." Instead, Carleton made clear, they could stay and starve, or go to New Mexico's Pecos River Valley.[46]

Carleton had big plans for Bosque Redondo, or "round forest" (the Diné called it Hwéeldi). He promised ample farmland. While the Diné learned "the art of peace" and "truths of Christianity," he said, "we gain for civilization their whole country, which is much larger in extent than the state of Ohio, and, besides being the best pastoral region between the two oceans, is said to abound in the precious as well as the useful metals." Instead, the move proved deadly. Over three years, up to two hundred died on the trail of up to four hundred miles. The army proved ill-equipped to aid them, and Mexican citizens who fought them harassed them en route.[47]

Reaching their destination was no help. It lacked the farmland and timber Carleton had promised and was too far from other reservations and forts to obtain them easily. In August 1864, he called the 7,500 Diné and Apache at Bosque Redondo "the happiest people I have ever seen." A month later, he referred to "hundreds of naked women and children . . . likely to perish." In October he fretted that "cold weather is setting in, and I have thousands of women and children who need the protection of a blanket." A freeze followed, killing what crops they could grow.[48]

The investigations prompted by the debacle cost Carleton his command. New Mexico superintendent of Indian affairs Michael Steck, a Lincoln appointee, originally backed him, but after realizing the extent of the failure he did his best to overturn "Fair Carletonia." Dole used the cost and broken promises to keep Indian Affairs in Interior, where it had been since the department's creation, and away from its old home in the War Department, where critics hoped to move it. Eventually, the War Department conceded that Bosque Redondo was a fiasco; the chiefs said, "If we were sent back, we would never commit an act of hostility. . . . We would go straight back the way we came." Historian Peter Iverson called the Treaty of Fort Sumner of 1868, which allowed them to do so, "a major turning point in Navajo history" that "attested to their determination to continue as a people." It also drove reform—after Lincoln died.[49]

### The Tribes of Abraham

While appointees in the Pacific Northwest were known as the "tribe of Abraham" for their links to Lincoln, similar ties existed throughout the West. Others owed their jobs to members of Congress loyal to Lincoln and his party. Indian superintendents and agents reported to Dole, another Illinoisan close to the president. Military appointees in the

West had fewer such claims on his friendship or time, but as part of the army they belonged to the branch that received most of his attention.

Their decisions affected Native Americans in varied ways. Evans, whom he knew in Illinois, was critical to the Sand Creek Massacre; Nye, who owed his job to Seward, tried to treat the Newe more fairly. Lincoln's appointees did nothing to abate the genocide in California that preceded his presidency, but Dole thought concentrating the state's Indigenous people would protect them, and by 1861 the most significant damage was done. A career military man instigated the "Long Walk of the Diné," a patronage appointee as superintendent of Indian affairs criticized him, and other Republicans investigated the results. The Diné returned to their land after negotiations with William Tecumseh Sherman, a general Lincoln admired, and Samuel Tappan, a member of an abolitionist family, who was appointed by Secretary of the Interior Orville Browning, once a close friend of Lincoln who had served with him in the Black Hawk War. While none of these was a true Indian reformer, their backgrounds suggest the varied attitudes and approaches.[50]

What happened in the West reflected several factors. One was the lack of easy communication: the distance from the Capitol made it harder for officials there to be involved in decision-making. Federal interest in the West lay in protecting mining and travel, making Native Americans not only less important but an economic threat. To condemn Lincoln for not understanding the horror of the Trail of Tears and the Long Walk is fair, but few then viewed these events as the disasters they were. Nor can Lincoln have been expected to know everything that happened two thousand miles from the Executive Mansion. But, as elsewhere, these were his appointees, supported by higher-level officials from his administration.

Lincoln's failures represented and reflected broader failures. He often was too tolerant of officials who ignored or belittled him, but he took no steps against his representatives in the West or in Indian Affairs. To Lincoln, Indigenous people in the West mattered less than white settlers and the capital they could generate. As the troubled Union tried to extend its empire and power westward, Americans saw Indigenous people as in the way, at the time and for decades to come.

# CONCLUSION

The many "might have beens" surrounding Abraham Lincoln often neglect Native Americans. Their importance (or lack of it) during his presidency becomes obvious in a search of his collected works, where many references are only to treaties sent to the Senate for ratification. Accordingly, this work often analyzes his appointees in a quest to understand what he thought and wanted, or extrapolate his lack of interest. How much would have changed if he had lived is hard to say. Native Americans became part and victims of the "Greater Reconstruction" that remade the nation, bringing together North, South, and West, often in ways Lincoln advocated.[1]

The military, no longer engaged in the Civil War, changed its focus. Leading this effort, Generals William Tecumseh Sherman and Phillip Sheridan disdained the West's Indigenous people. Their job was to help Republicans achieve their goals in the Homestead and Pacific Railroad acts: whites building and settling the West. That meant stopping Indian interference and depriving them of their land and influence.[2]

Civil rights laws also affected Native Americans. In 1866, as Congress defined African American rights, Native Americans' rights were reduced. The Fourteenth Amendment's exemption of "Indians not taxed" from citizenship fit the pattern by eliminating any chance of Native Americans having a political voice or impact on their own. As Stephen Kantrowitz put it, "From the vantage point of anti-extensionist settler colonialism, the Civil War was largely a story of continuity." Senator Lyman Trumbull of Illinois called the Native Americans "a class of persons . . . not regarded as part of our people" when he wrote the Civil Rights Act of 1866, the basis for the amendment. Congress banned peonage and slavery in New Mexico in 1867—the year it instituted military reconstruction across the South. Ironically, by going west with the army, African Americans continued the wartime process of convincing some Americans they were worthy citizens, and they did so by helping to subjugate Native Americans.[3]

When Ulysses Grant became president in 1869, he sought a "Peace Policy" toward Native Americans. His inaugural address urged "proper treatment of the original occupants of this land" and "any course toward them which tends to their civilization and ultimate citizenship," reflecting reformist views and cultural disdain. He named one of his former military staff, General Ely Parker, a Seneca, commissioner of Indian affairs and worked closely with him on the issue. Contrary to what many Indigenous people argued, however, Parker asserted, "The Indian tribes of the United States are not sovereign nations." In 1871 Congress declared, "Hereafter no Indian nation or tribe within the territory of the United States shall be acknowledged or recognized as an independent nation, tribe, or power with whom the United States may contract by treaty." The government took the opportunities presented by its expanded power during Reconstruction to deny Native sovereignty—and eventually scaled back protections and sovereignty for African Americans while accepting white sovereignty in the former Confederacy.[4]

Yet Grant legitimately sought reform. He supported creating a Board of Indian Commissioners to advise the federal government, but the group accomplished little. He and other reformers hoped to eliminate patronage problems by appointing Christian missionaries to run reservations. But they still supported assimilation and eliminating Native culture, including the buffalo herds that Natives depended on. As with Reconstruction, several factors (from the Panic of 1873, bigotry, and gold discoveries that inspired increased settlement to continuing Indian wars and Congress trying to maintain patronage jobs) undercut and ultimately ruined the Peace Policy.[5]

Whether Lincoln would have tried something similar is unknowable. Had he sought reform, his political skills might have made it a success. When prosperity returned in the late 1870s and early 1880s and a spate of railroad-building began, Congress gave entrepreneurs the right-of-way across Indian Territory under its power of eminent domain. Ironically, Lincoln's signature on the Pacific Railroad Act of 1862 was the opening salvo in destroying Native society in the far West for the sake of railroads. Although the Dawes Severalty Act of 1887 reversed the concentration that his administration advocated, it reflected the goal of assimilating Native Americans into Anglo society and was suggestive of the Homestead Act, which Lincoln and Dawes had supported a quarter of a century before.[6]

Yet as Reconstruction wound down, Indian reform gained ground. Rutherford Hayes's inauguration in 1877 marked a turning point in Republican involvement in southern affairs. But his interior secretary, onetime German revolutionary and Civil War general and diplomat Carl Schurz, tried to reform the Bureau of Indian Affairs and fended off War Department attempts to take it over—as Lincoln's appointees did.[7]

Any examination of Lincoln and Native Americans reveals much that should disturb his fans. William Freehling wrote of his support for black colonization in eulogizing Henry Clay, "No Lincoln utterance more inspires modern shudders." When Lincoln began his fourth debate with Stephen Douglas in 1858 by announcing that he was not "in favor of producing a perfect equality between the negroes and white people," Allen Guelzo called these "the words every Lincoln admirer since then wishes he had never uttered." Neither of them is wrong, but while Lincoln advanced considerably in his thinking about African Americans, Native Americans were another matter. He approved a mass execution, said nothing about massacres, had no conversations with Indigenous people that rivaled the respect he demonstrated for African Americans, stalled Indian reformers, and thought it necessary to explain the planet to a delegation of chiefs. He put economic growth ahead of those who had lived in the West for generations, and he denied their heritage by supporting taking their land and concentrating them. He encouraged a free labor ideology for white Americans and sought to extend it to African Americans, but he saw no place in it for Native Americans.[8]

But a litany of condemnation is unfair to Lincoln. To expect him to live outside of his time would be ahistorical: few sympathized enough with Native peoples to promote major changes in policy, certainly in comparison with advocates of African American rights. To demand empathy from him is to fall into the trap of expecting him to be better than others when historians have lamented the belief among his more devoted admirers that he started out perfect and improved with time. As a smart politician, he knew the risks of fighting too hard on behalf of Native Americans, capturing that problem when he said that he could not hang men for votes, and when his commutation of so many Dakota drew more criticism for its humanity than for its cruelty. As David Nichols, the leading scholar on the subject, wrote, "His sympathies for Indians, however genuine, never altered his priorities for the development he deemed essential to the prosecution of the Civil War and the nation's destiny." But "it is difficult to see how Lincoln could have chosen any alternative path acceptable to his European-American constituency and the extraordinary circumstances of Civil War."[9]

Indeed, Lincoln's and his party's free labor ideology succeeded more in the West than in the South. The formerly enslaved in the South after Reconstruction and the West's original inhabitants both faced injustice. As white Northerners and Southerners moved west, they brought their biases with them. When they farmed or worked in industry, they did so on land that had belonged to Native peoples, who were concentrated on reservations and then expected to do what many whites and African Americans had not done and leave their culture completely behind them. If free labor was the Republican solution for white people, and then for African Americans, it was a different matter for Native Americans. The ideology of settler colonialism, which they did not voice, mattered more.[10]

Lincoln had a complex view of and relationship with Indians. The son of victims of tribes fighting white encroachment, he joined a war against tribes fighting white encroachment, supported policies that made matters worse, and led the country in a war that helped expand white settlement. Although ignorant of Native customs, he revealed none of the hatred for their culture that animated other leaders and some of his political and military officials. In this regard he was better than many of his contemporaries, and presidential predecessors and successors, but not what his admirers or those who wanted better lives for Native Americans would have liked him to be.

# ACKNOWLEDGMENTS

I have much gratitude to express, starting with Richard Etulain and Sylvia Rodrigue, friends and editors of this series whom I was blessed to work with for a book on the 1860 election, and in contributing to Dick's volume on Lincoln and the West. They made this work possible and better.

Historians could not survive without librarians and archivists, and those at the University of Nevada, Las Vegas, and the Huntington Library in particular have been wonderful. I presented some of these conclusions to the Western History Association and thank panelists Megan Kate Nelson, Daniel Sharfstein, and Scott Stabler for friendship and support. Michael Birkner, Randall Miller, and John Quist invited me to contribute to *The Worlds of James Buchanan and Thaddeus Stevens*, and addressing Stevens on the West helped inform my thinking on Lincoln. Friends who are better scholars of Native Americans than I am—especially William Bauer and Sondra Cosgrove—helped, as have outstanding graduate students: Bridger Bishop, Neil Dodge, Bridget Groat, Lee Hanover, and especially Shae Cox; our discussions, on this and other topics, aided me, whether or not they (or I) knew it at the time before they headed off to outdo whatever I have done (Drs. Cox and Groat are now tenure-track faculty; the others will be). Undergraduates in my course on Lincoln similarly influenced me. The friendship of Jeff Schauer (and discussions of colonialism and diplomacy) and Jill Acree (who led me through the Parson Weems thicket) means a lot. Andy Fry and David Tanenhaus read the manuscript and were as thoughtful in their critiques as they are dedicated in their friendship.

Many friends inside and outside my profession have offered encouragement and assistance through the years. I will single out DeAnna Beachley, Jonathan Birnbaum, Eric Foner, Yanek Mieczkowski, Heather Richardson, John David Smith, Michael Vorenberg, and Xi Wang, and the Denton, Foley, and Roske families, but I could name many more.

My wife, Deborah Young, gives me love and support I do not claim to deserve, but I am glad to say it again and thank our relatives and friends for their support.

The dedication reflects some other debts I owe. UNLV, where I was a student and now am a faculty member, has been a welcoming and happy place to work; Andy Fry has been one of my mentors and dearest friends, and our colleagues have been teachers as well as friends. I am grateful to friends and advisers at Columbia University, where I earned my PhD and studied Euro–Native American relations under Alden Vaughan's wise and kindly tutelage.

As I finished this book, my father Robert Green and UNLV history professor Gene Moehring died. They taught me a lot, directly and indirectly, by action and example. Tennyson wrote in "Ulysses," "I am a part of all that I have met." These four men have done much to shape the better parts of me.

# NOTES

## Introduction

1. George M. Fredrickson, *Big Enough to Be Inconsistent: Abraham Lincoln Confronts Slavery and Race* (Cambridge, MA: Harvard University Press, 2008); Eric Foner, *The Fiery Trial: Abraham Lincoln and American Slavery* (New York: W. W. Norton, 2010), 261–63; Phillip Paludan, *The Presidency of Abraham Lincoln* (Lawrence: University Press of Kansas, 1994), 117; David Herbert Donald, *Lincoln* (New York: Simon & Schuster, 1995); Michael Burlingame, *Abraham Lincoln: A Life*, 2 vols. (Baltimore: Johns Hopkins University Press, 2008).

2. David A. Nichols, *Lincoln and the Indians: Civil War Policy and Politics* (1978; repr., St. Paul: Minnesota Historical Society Press, 2012).

3. Nell Irvin Painter, *The History of White People* (New York: W. W. Norton, 2010), ix; Brian DeLay, "Indian Politics, Empire, and the History of American Foreign Relations," *Diplomatic History* 39, no. 5 (November 2015): 927–42; Alexandra Harmon, "American Indians, American Law, and Modern American Foreign Relations," *Diplomatic History* 39, no. 5 (November 2015): 943–54.

4. Patrick Wolfe, "Settler Colonialism and the Elimination of the Native," *Journal of Genocide Research* 8, no. 4 (December 2006): 387–409, at 388, 396; Walter L. Hixson, *American Settler Colonialism: A History* (New York: Palgrave Macmillan, 2013), esp. 9–20; Eugene P. Moehring, *Urbanism and Empire in the Far West: 1840–1890* (Reno: University of Nevada Press, 2004), xxiii; Gary Clayton Anderson, *Ethnic Cleansing and the Indian: The Crime That Should Haunt America* (Norman: University of Oklahoma Press, 2014); John P. Bowes, *Black Hawk and the War of 1832: Removal in the North* (New York: Chelsea House, 2007), 12.

5. Roger Long, ed., *The Man on the Spot: Essays on British Empire History* (Westport, CT: Praeger, 1995); John S. Galbraith, *Reluctant Empire: British Policy on the South African Frontier, 1834–1854* (Westport, CT: Greenwood, 1963). The newest history of Sand Creek is Louis Kraft, *Sand Creek and the Tragic End of a Lifeway* (Norman: University of Oklahoma Press, 2020).

## 1. Beginnings

1. Alden T. Vaughan, "From White Man to Redskin: Changing Anglo-American Perceptions of the American Indian," *American Historical Review* 87, no. 4 (October 1982): 917–19.

2. *National Intelligencer*, January 12, 1830; Abraham Lincoln, "First Debate with Stephen A. Douglas at Ottawa, Illinois," August 21, 1858, in

Debates Scrapbook, Lincoln ms., Library of Congress, *The Collected Works of Abraham Lincoln*, ed. Roy P. Basler, 9 vols. (New Brunswick, NJ: Rutgers University Press, 1953–55), 3:30; Christopher W. Anderson, "Native Americans and the Origins of Abraham Lincoln's Views on Race," *Journal of the Abraham Lincoln Association* 37, no. 1 (Spring 2016): 11–29. See also Jason Emerson, *Lincoln the Inventor* (Carbondale: Southern Illinois University Press, 2009); Lincoln, "Autobiography Written for John L. Scripps," c. June 1860, *Collected Works*, 4:62.

3. Lincoln, "Autobiography," in Lincoln to Jesse W. Fell, Springfield, December 20, 1859, *Collected Works*, 3:511.

4. Michael Burlingame, *Abraham Lincoln: A Life*, 2 vols. (Baltimore: Johns Hopkins University Press, 2008), 1:1–2; Brian Dirck, *Lincoln in Indiana* (Carbondale: Southern Illinois University Press, 2017), 22; H. E. Robinson, "The Lincoln, Hanks, and Boone Families," *Missouri Historical Review* 1, no. 1 (October 1906): 72–84; T. H. Breen, *Puritans and Adventurers: Change and Persistence in Early America* (New York: Oxford University Press, 1980), 65, 75–76; David Grayson Allen, *In English Ways: The Movement of Societies and the Transferal of English Local Law and Custom to Massachusetts Bay in the Seventeenth Century* (New York: W. W. Norton, 1982), 55–81; David Hackett Fischer, *Albion's Seed: Four British Folkways in America* (New York: Oxford University Press, 1989), 805.

5. Alden T. Vaughan, *New England Frontier: Puritans and Indians, 1620–1675* (Boston: Little, Brown, 1965), 60, 291–92, 314–16; William Cronon, *Changes in the Land: Indians, Colonists, and the Ecology of New England* (New York: Hill & Wang, 1983), 85–91. See Laurence M. Hauptman, *Between Two Fires: American Indians and the Civil War* (New York: Free Press, 1995), 147–48; Katherine A. Grandjean, "New World Tempests: Environment, Scarcity, and the Coming of the Pequot War," *William and Mary Quarterly* 68, no. 1 (Spring 2011): 75–100.

6. Burlingame, *Lincoln*, 1:1–2; Louis A. Warren, "The Lincolns of Berks County," *Historical Review of Berks County* 14 (April 1949): 83–85, http://www.berkshistory.org/multimedia/articles/the-lincolns-of-berks-county; *Reading Eagle*, March 6, 1927, https://news.google.com/newspapers?id=x5IhAAAAIBAJ&sjid=JpgFAAAAIBAJ&pg=3474%2C1036348; Elizabeth Brown Pryor, *Six Encounters with Lincoln: A President Confronts Democracy and Its Demons* (New York: Penguin, 2018), 375, n. 38; Charles H. Coleman, "Lincoln's Lincoln Grandmother," *Journal of the Illinois State Historical Society* 52, no. 1 (Spring 1959): 59–90. On early Pennsylvania, see Alan Taylor, *American Colonies* (New York: Penguin, 2001).

7. Burlingame, *Lincoln*, 1:1–2; James Corbett David, *Dunmore's New World: The Extraordinary Life of a Royal Governor in Revolutionary*

*America—with Jacobites, Counterfeiters, Land Schemes, Shipwrecks, Scalping, Indian Politics, Runaway Slaves, and Two Illegal Royal Weddings* (Charlottesville: University of Virginia Press, 2013); Harvey Jackson, *Lachlan McIntosh and the Politics of Revolutionary Georgia* (Athens: University of Georgia Press, 1979).

8. Patricia Watlington, "Discontent in Frontier Kentucky," *Register of the Kentucky Historical Society* 65, no. 2 (April 1967): 77–93; A. H. Chapman, Written Statement, in Douglas L. Wilson and Rodney O. Davis, eds., *Herndon's Informants: Letters, Interviews, and Statements about Abraham Lincoln* (Urbana: University of Illinois Press, 1998), 95–96; Louis Warren, *Lincoln's Youth: Indiana Years, Seven to Twenty-One, 1816–1830* (Indianapolis: Indiana Historical Society, 1959), 33; Stephen Aron, "The Significance of the Kentucky Frontier," *Register of the Kentucky Historical Society* 91, no. 3 (Summer 1993): 298–323; John Mack Faragher, *Daniel Boone: The Life and Legend of an American Pioneer* (New York: Henry Holt, 1992), 201–12; Donald, *Lincoln,* 21.

9. Dennis Hanks to William Henry Herndon, Chicago, June 13, 1865, in Wilson and Davis, *Herndon's Informants*, 36; Chapman, Written Statement, in ibid., 95–96; Augustus H. Chapman, Herndon Interview, 1865 or 1866, in ibid., 439; John Hanks, Herndon Interview, 1865 or 1866, in ibid., 453–54; Waldo Lincoln, *History of the Lincoln Family: An Account of the Descendants of Samuel Lincoln, of Hingham, Massachusetts, 1637–1920* (Worcester, MA: Commonwealth Press, 1923), 130.

10. Hanks to Herndon, Chicago, June 13, 1865, in Wilson and Davis, *Herndon's Informants*, 36; Chapman, Written Statement, in ibid., 95–96; William Clagett Statement, n.d., in ibid., 220.

11. Burlingame, *Lincoln*, 1:3; Thomas L. D. Johnston, Herndon Interview, ca. 1866, in Wilson and Davis, *Herndon's Informants*, 533; Warren, *Lincoln's Youth*, 34.

12. Hanks to Herndon, Chicago, June 13, 1865, in Wilson and Davis, *Herndon's Informants*, 36; Douglas L. Wilson, *Honor's Voice: The Transformation of Abraham Lincoln* (New York: Alfred A. Knopf, 1998), 19–52.

13. Benjamin P. Thomas, *Abraham Lincoln: A Biography* (New York: Alfred A. Knopf, 1952), 6; Caroline Hanks Hitchcock, *Nancy Hanks: The Story of Abraham Lincoln's Mother* (New York: Doubleday & McClure, 1900); "Hanks," Family Tree DNA, https://www.familytreedna.com/public /HanksDNAProject/default.aspx?section=news; Helen C. Rountree, *The Powhatan Indians of Virginia: Their Traditional Culture* (Norman: University of Oklahoma Press, 1989), 89–143.

14. "Hanks," Family Tree DNA, https://www.familytreedna.com/public /HanksDNAProject/default.aspx?section=news; *Louisville Courier-Journal*, December 5, 1909, https://bullittcountyhistory.org/bchistory /lastindianfight.html.

15. Warren, *Lincoln's Youth*, 7–8, 34; Richard Lawrence Miller, *Lincoln and His World: The Early Years: Birth to Illinois Legislature* (Mechanicsburg, PA: Stackpole Books, 2006), 5; Louis A. Warren, "The Romance of Thomas Lincoln and Nancy Hanks," *Indiana Magazine of History* 30, no. 3 (September 1934): 213–22.

16. Warren, *Lincoln's Youth*, 35.

17. Brian Dirck, "Lincoln's Kentucky Childhood and Race," *Register of the Kentucky Historical Society* 106, nos. 3–4 (Summer/Autumn 2008): 321–24.

18. Fred Kaplan, *Lincoln: The Biography of a Writer* (New York: Harper Collins, 2008), 25–27.

19. Douglas L. Wilson, *Lincoln before Washington: New Perspectives on the Illinois Years* (Urbana: University of Illinois Press, 1998), 6–7; Ralph D. Gray, ed., *Indiana History: A Book of Readings* (Bloomington: Indiana University Press, 1994), 11–12; Benjamin Franklin, *The Autobiography of Benjamin Franklin* (Boston: Houghton Mifflin, 1896), 150–51; Hanks Interview with Herndon, Chicago, June 13, 1865, in Wilson and Davis, *Herndon's Informants*, 39. Michael Burlingame questions whether Lincoln read Franklin's autobiography; Burlingame, *Lincoln*, 1:36.

20. Marcus L. Cunliffe, ed., *The Life of Washington by Mason L. Weems* (Cambridge, MA: Harvard University Press, 1962), 31; Jill Acree, "The Sorrows of Parson Weems: His Life and Legacy" (PhD diss., Claremont Graduate University, 2007); David Ramsay, *The Life of George Washington: Commander in Chief of the Armies of the United States of America, Throughout the War which Established Their Independence, and First President of the United States*, ed. William Grimshaw (Baltimore: Joseph Jewitt and Cushing & Sons, 1832), 9–10, 90, 187, 189; Colin G. Calloway, *The Indian World of George Washington: The First President, the First Americans, and the Birth of the Nation* (New York: Oxford University Press, 2018).

21. A. T. Lowe, *The Columbian Class Book: Consisting of Geographical, Historical, and Biographical Extracts. . . .* , 4th ed. (Worcester, MA: Dorr & Howland, 1829), 58–60; Caleb Bingham, *The American Preceptor; Being a New Selection of Lessons for Reading and Speaking. Designed for the Use of Schools* (Boston: Manning & Loring, 1811), 88–89; Robert Bray, *Reading with Lincoln* (Carbondale: Southern Illinois University Press, 2010), 10; Robert Bray, "What Abraham Lincoln Read—an Evaluative and Annotated List," *Journal of the Abraham Lincoln Association* 28, no. 2 (Summer 2007): 28–81.

22. Joshua Speed to Herndon, December 6, 1866, in Wilson and Davis, *Herndon's Informants*, 499; J. Rowan Herndon to Herndon, Quincy, May 28, 1865, in ibid., 7; Donald, *Lincoln*, 145.

23. John D. Barnhart and Dorothy L. Riker, *Indiana to 1816: The Colonial Period* (Indianapolis: Indiana Historical Bureau and Indiana Historical Society, 1971), 370–77, 401; Hanks to Herndon, n.p., May 4, 1866, in Wilson and Davis, *Herndon's Informants*, 251; Andrew R. L. Cayton, *Frontier Indiana* (Bloomington: Indiana University Press, 1996), 272; Burlingame, *Lincoln*, 1:19–20.

24. Alec R. Gilpin, *The War of 1812 in the Old Northwest* (East Lansing: Michigan State University Press, 1958); Robert M. Owens, *Mr. Jefferson's Hammer: William Henry Harrison and the Origins of American Indian Policy* (Norman: University of Oklahoma Press, 2007), 166–239.

25. Lincoln, "Copybook Verses" [1824–1826], *Collected Works*, 1:1–2; Elizabeth Crawford to Herndon, April 19, 1866, in Wilson and Davis, *Herndon's Informants*, 245.

26. Warren, *Lincoln's Youth*, 203–15; Donald, *Lincoln*, 36–39; Burlingame, *Lincoln*, 1:48–57.

27. Gillum Ferguson, *Illinois in the War of 1812* (Urbana: University of Illinois Press, 2012).

## 2. Militias and Mosquitoes

1. Michael Paul Rogin, *Fathers and Children: Andrew Jackson and the Subjugation of the American Indian* (New York: Random House, 1975), 234–35; Daniel Walker Howe, *What Hath God Wrought: The Transformation of America, 1815–1848* (New York: Oxford University Press, 2007), 418–20; Roger L. Nichols, *Black Hawk and the Warrior's Path* (Arlington Heights, IL: Harlan Davidson, 1992), 1–66.

2. J. D. Patterson, ed., *Life of Ma-Ka-Tai-Me-She-Kia-Kiak or Black Hawk . . .* (Cincinnati: Russell, Odiorne & Metcalf, 1834), 105–6 and passim; Rogin, *Fathers and Children*, 234–35; Howe, *What Hath God Wrought*, 418–20; Benjamin P. Thomas, *Lincoln's New Salem*, rev. ed. (Chicago: Americana House, 1951), 77; Nichols, *Black Hawk*, 66–100; Burlingame, *Lincoln*, 1:67–71; John P. Bowes, *Black Hawk and the War of 1832: Removal in the North* (New York: Chelsea House, 2007), 44. See John W. Hall, *Uncommon Defense: Indian Allies in the Black Hawk War* (Cambridge, MA: Harvard University Press, 2009); Patrick J. Jung, *The Black Hawk War of 1832* (Norman: University of Oklahoma Press, 2007); Kerry A. Trask, *Black Hawk: The Battle for the Heart of America* (New York: Henry Holt, 2007).

3. Patterson, *Black Hawk*, 134–36; Thomas, *Lincoln's New Salem*, 77–78; Nichols, *Black Hawk*, 101–35; Trask, *Black Hawk*, 296, 303; Rogin, *Fathers and Children*, 234–35; Harry L. Watson, *Liberty and Power: The Politics of Jacksonian America*, 2nd ed. (New York: Hill & Wang, 2006), 104–13.

4. Howe, *What Hath God Wrought*, 418–20.

5. Thomas, *Lincoln's New Salem*, 79–83; William G. Greene to William Henry Herndon, June 11, 1865, in Wilson and Davis, *Herndon's Informants*, 33.

6. Thomas, *Lincoln's New Salem*, 77–78; Charles B. Strozier, *Lincoln's Quest for Union: Public and Private Meanings* (New York: Basic Books, 1982), 32, and 241, n. 8; Thomas, *Lincoln*, 33, 37; Donald, *Lincoln*, 44–46. Donald wrote that "men rushed to offer their services, some out of patriotism, some out of long-cherished animosity toward Indians, and some who knew that military service would aid their political careers. In Lincoln's case all these motives were at work," yet the record shows no "animosity" on his part.

7. Thomas, *Lincoln's New Salem*, 82; Royal Clary, Interview with Herndon, ca. October 1866, in Wilson and Davis, *Herndon's Informants*, 372; George M. Harrison to Herndon, ca. 1866, in ibid., 327–29; Benjamin F. Irwin to Herndon, September 22, 1866, in ibid., 353; Jung, *Black Hawk War*, 81–82; Douglas L. Wilson, *Honor's Voice: The Transformation of Abraham Lincoln* (New York: Alfred A. Knopf, 1998), 6–7.

8. Lincoln to Jesse W. Fell, Springfield, December 20, 1859, *Collected Works*, 3:512; Burlingame, *Lincoln*, 1:67; Thomas, *Lincoln's New Salem*, 78, n. 5.

9. Wilson, *Honor's Voice*, 29–30, 48–49; Thomas, *Lincoln's New Salem*, 78–81; David M. Pantier to Herndon, Petersburg, July 21, 1865, in Wilson and Davis, *Herndon's Informants*, 78. Burlingame provides a slightly different quotation from a different source in *Abraham Lincoln*, 1:67.

10. Trask, *Black Hawk*, 163; Thomas, *Lincoln's New Salem*, 80; Greene to Herndon, Elm Wood, May 30, 1865, in Wilson and Davis, *Herndon's Informants*, 18–19; Greene to Herndon, Home, November 1, 1866, in ibid., 390; Royal Clary, Herndon Interview, ca. October 1866, in ibid., 370–72; Nichols, *Lincoln and the Indians*, 3–4; Thomas A. Horrocks, *Lincoln's Campaign Biographies* (Carbondale: Southern Illinois University Press, 2014).

11. J. Rowan Herndon to Herndon, Quincy, May 28, 1865, in Wilson and Davis, *Herndon's Informants*, 6–7; Greene to Herndon, Elm Wood, May 30, 1865, in ibid., 18–19; George M. Harrison to Herndon, Richland, January 29, 1867, in ibid., 553–54; Thomas, *Lincoln's New Salem*, 82–83; Wilson, *Honor's Voice*, 29.

12. Thomas, *Lincoln's New Salem*, 84; Harrison to Herndon, Richland, January 29, 1867, in Wilson and Davis, *Herndon's Informants*, 555; Henry McHenry, Herndon Interview, Petersburg, May 29, 1865, in ibid., 15; Frank J. Williams, *Judging Lincoln* (Carbondale: Southern Illinois University Press, 2002), 149; Nichols, *Lincoln and the Indians*, 3; Don E. Fehrenbacher, *Prelude to Greatness: Lincoln in the 1850s* (Stanford, CA:

Stanford University Press, 1962), 27–28; Sidney Blumenthal, *A Self-Made Man: The Political Life of Abraham Lincoln*, vol. 1, *1809–1849* (New York: Simon & Schuster, 2016); Ron J. Keller, *Lincoln and the Illinois Legislature* (Carbondale: Southern Illinois University Press, 2019), 10–13.

13. Thomas, *Lincoln's New Salem*, 84; Wilson, *Honor's Voice*, 10; Williams, *Judging Lincoln*, 35–36, 95–96; Thomas, *Lincoln*, 33–34; Kaplan, *Lincoln*, 58; Trask, *Black Hawk*, 296–97; Donald, *Lincoln*, 44–46.

14. Nichols, *Lincoln and the Indians*, 4.

15. Lincoln to Jesse W. Fell, Springfield, December 20, 1859, *Collected Works*, 3:512; Howe, *What Hath God Wrought*, 62, 597; Joel H. Silbey, "'Always a Whig in Politics': The Partisan Life of Abraham Lincoln," *Journal of the Abraham Lincoln Association* 8, no. 1 (1996): 21–42.

16. See Michael F. Holt, *The Rise and Fall of the American Whig Party: Jacksonian Politics and the Onset of Civil War* (New York: Oxford University Press, 1999).

17. Lincoln, "Open Letter on Springfield and Alton Railroad," June 30, 1847, *Collected Works*, 1:397–98; Howe, *What Hath God Wrought*, 584–85; Merrill D. Peterson, *The Great Triumvirate: Webster, Clay, and Calhoun* (New York: Oxford University Press, 1987), 196; Blumenthal, *Self-Made Man*, 70.

18. Andrew Jackson to John C. Calhoun, Nashville, September 2, 1820, in Harold D. Moser, David R. Hoth, and George H. Hoemann, eds., *The Papers of Andrew Jackson*, vol. 4, *1816–1820* (Knoxville: University of Tennessee Press, 1994), 388; Peterson, *Great Triumvirate*, 90–92.

19. John Fitzpatrick, ed., *The Autobiography of Martin Van Buren*, vol. 2 of the 1918 Annual Report of the American Historical Association (Washington, DC: Government Printing Office, 1920,), 295; Peterson, *Great Triumvirate*, 195; Howe, *What Hath God Wrought*, 347.

20. George D. Prentice, *Biography of Henry Clay*, 2nd ed. (New York: John Jay Phelps, 1831), 162–67; Blumenthal, *Self-Made Man*, 62.

21. Watson, *Liberty and Power*, 53–54; "On Our Relations with the Cherokee Indians," February 4, 1835, in Calvin Colton, ed., *The Speeches of Henry Clay*, 2 vols. (New York: A. S. Barnes, 1857), 1:655; Robert V. Remini, *Henry Clay: Statesman for the Union* (New York: W. W. Norton, 1991), 314–15; Ronald N. Satz, *American Indian Policy in the Jacksonian Era* (Lincoln: University of Nebraska Press, 1975), 39–53, 86, 160–64, 192–96; Rickey L. Hendricks, "Henry Clay and Jacksonian Indian Policy: A Political Anachronism," *Filson Club History Quarterly* 60, no. 1 (April 1986): 218–38.

22. Thomas Brown, *Politics and Statesmanship: Essays on the American Whig Party* (New York: Columbia University Press, 1985), 264, n. 53; Satz, *Jacksonian Era*, 40, 52. On colonization, see Michael Vorenberg, "Abraham Lincoln and the Politics of Black Colonization," *Journal of the*

*Abraham Lincoln Association* 142 (Summer 1993): 22–45; Eric Foner, "Lincoln and Colonization," in Foner, ed., *Our Lincoln: New Perspectives on Lincoln and His World* (New York: W. W. Norton, 2008), 135–66. See Remini, *Henry Clay*, 179, 395, 484, 507–08, 797; James Lander, *Lincoln and Darwin: Shared Visions of Race, Science, and Religion* (Carbondale: Southern Illinois University Press, 2010), 187, 191–92; Nichols, *Lincoln and the Indians*, 190–91.

23. Lincoln, "Protest in Illinois Legislature on Slavery," March 3, 1837, *Collected Works*, 1:74–75; Lincoln to Williamson Durley, Springfield, October 3, 1845, in ibid., 1:347–48; Natalie Joy, "The Indian's Cause: Abolitionists and Native American Rights," *Journal of the Civil War Era* 8, no. 2 (June 2018): 215–42.

24. On Illinois, see Graham A. Peck, *Making an Antislavery Nation: Lincoln, Douglas, and the Battle over Freedom* (Baton Rouge: Louisiana State University Press, 2017).

25. Jean Harvey Baker, *Mary Todd Lincoln: A Biography* (New York: W. W. Norton, 1987); Catherine Clinton, *Mrs. Lincoln: A Life* (New York: HarperCollins, 2009).

26. John Mack Faragher, *Daniel Boone: The Life and Legend of an American Pioneer* (New York: Henry Holt, 1992), 217–24; Michael C. C. Adams, "An Appraisal of the Blue Licks Battle," *Filson Club Historical Quarterly* 75, no. 2 (Summer 2001): 181–203.

27. "The Law Practice of Abraham Lincoln," 2nd ed., The Papers of Abraham Lincoln, www.lawpracticeofabrahamlincoln.org, Todd et al. v. Wickliffe; Sidney Blumenthal, *Wrestling with His Angel: The Political Life of Abraham Lincoln*, vol. 2, *1849–1856* (New York: Simon & Schuster, 2017), 9–40.

28. Kenneth J. Winkle, *Abraham and Mary Lincoln* (Carbondale: Southern Illinois University Press, 2011), 16–18.

29. Lincoln, "Speech on the Sub-Treasury," December 26, 1839, *Collected Works*, 1:173–75.

30. Ibid.

31. Ibid.

32. Joel H. Silbey, *Party over Section: The Rough and Ready Presidential Election of 1848* (Lawrence: University Press of Kansas, 2009).

33. Lincoln, *Congressional Globe*, 31st Congress, 1st Session, July 27, 1848, Appendix, 1041–43, *Collected Works*, 1:501–16, at 509–10; Richard Carwardine, *Lincoln's Sense of Humor* (Carbondale: Southern Illinois University Press, 2017), 22.

34. Lincoln, *Congressional Globe*, 31st Congress, 1st Session, July 27, 1848, Appendix, 1041–43, *Collected Works*, 1:501–16; Lincoln to Thomas Ewing, Springfield, March 22, 1850, in ibid., 2, 78.

35. Lincoln to Jesse W. Fell, Springfield, December 20, 1859, *Collected Works*, 3:512.

36. Lincoln, "First Lecture on Discoveries and Inventions," April 6, 1858, *Collected Works*, 2:440.

37. Lincoln, "Address before the Wisconsin State Agricultural Society," Milwaukee, September 30, 1859, *Collected Works*, 3:478–79; Lincoln, "Speech at Carlinville, Illinois," August 31, 1858, in ibid., 3:81; Eric Foner, *Free Soil, Free Labor, Free Men: The Ideology of the Republican Party before the Civil War*, reprint ed. (New York: Oxford University Press, 1995), xxvii.

### 3. People, Policy, and Bureaucracy

1. Charles Francis Adams Diary, March 12, 28, and 31, 1861, Massachusetts Historical Society (microfilm); Richard Brookhiser, *America's Dynasty: The Adamses* (New York: Free Press, 2002), 131.

2. George E. Baker, ed., *The Works of William H. Seward*, 5 vols. (Boston: Houghton Mifflin, 1853–1884), 4:363; Joseph A. Fry, *Lincoln, Seward, and US Foreign Relations in the Civil War Era* (Lexington: University Press of Kentucky, 2019); Paul Kahan, *Amiable Scoundrel: Simon Cameron, Lincoln's Scandalous Secretary of War* (Lincoln: University of Nebraska Press, 2016), 29–40.

3. Republican Party Platforms, Republican Party Platform of 1860 Online by Gerhard Peters and John T. Woolley, American Presidency Project, https://www.presidency.ucsb.edu/node/273296; Vincent G. Tegeder, "Lincoln and Territorial Patronage: The Ascendancy of the Radicals in the West," *Mississippi Valley Historical Review* 35, no. 2 (June 1948): 77–90; Harry Carman and Reinhard J. Luthin, *Lincoln and the Patronage* (New York: Columbia University Press, 1943).

4. William Henry Perrin, *The History of Edgar County, Illinois. . . .* (Chicago: William Le Baron Jr., 1879), 569–70; Daniel W. Wilder to William Henry Herndon, Rochester, November 26, 1866, in Wilson and Davis, *Herndon's Informants*, 419; Nichols, *Lincoln and the Indians*, 21; Elmo R. Richardson and Alan W. Farley, *John Palmer Usher: Lincoln's Secretary of the Interior* (Lawrence: University Press of Kansas, 1960).

5. Nichols, *Lincoln and the Indians*, 186; Joshua Zeitz, *Lincoln's Boys: John Hay, John Nicolay, and the War for Lincoln's Image* (New York: Penguin, 2014); Michael Burlingame, ed., *With Lincoln in the White House: Letters, Memoranda, and Other Writings of John G. Nicolay, 1860–1865* (Carbondale: Southern Illinois University Press, 2006).

6. *New York Tribune*, December 25 and 26, 1860; [Keene] *New Hampshire Sentinel*, August 1, 1861; *New York Herald*, January 3, 1861; Mark W. Summers, *The Plundering Generation: Corruption and the Crisis of the Union, 1849–1861* (New York: Oxford University Press, 1987).

7. Edmond Danziger Jr., *Indians and Bureaucrats: Administering the Reservation Policy during the Civil War* (Urbana: University of Illinois Press, 1974), 15; Nichols, *Lincoln and the Indians*, 15–20.

8. Danziger, *Indians and Bureaucrats*, 15–16.

9. Nichols, *Lincoln and the Indians*, 20–21; *Report of the Special Joint Committee on the Condition of the Indian Tribes*, 39th Congress, 2nd Session (Washington, DC: Government Printing Office, 1867).

10. Robert W. Johannsen, "The Tribe of Abraham: Lincoln and the Washington Territory," in Richard W. Etulain, ed., *Lincoln Looks West: From the Mississippi to the Pacific* (Carbondale: Southern Illinois University Press, 2010), 164; Nichols, *Lincoln and the Indians*, 6; *Congressional Globe*, 37th Congress, 2nd Session, June 2, 1862, 2477; Danziger, *Indians and Bureaucrats*, 162–64.

11. Anson G. Henry to William P. Dole, Olympia, October 28, 1861, Abraham Lincoln Papers, Series 1, Correspondence, 1833–1916, Library of Congress; Robert E. Ficken, *Washington Territory* (Pullman: Washington State University Press, 2002), 63–66; Richard W. Etulain, *Lincoln and Oregon Country Politics in the Civil War Era* (Corvallis: Oregon State University Press, 2013), 91–93.

12. Henry to Lincoln, Olympia, October 17, 1862, Abraham Lincoln Papers, Series 1, Correspondence, 1833–1916, Library of Congress.

13. James Short to Lincoln, San Francisco, January 17, 1864, in ibid.; Stacey L. Smith, *Freedom's Frontier: California and the Struggle over Unfree Labor, Emancipation, and Reconstruction* (Chapel Hill: University of North Carolina Press, 2013), 186–89.

14. Nichols, *Lincoln and the Indians*, 18, 70, 123; Danziger, *Indians and Bureaucrats*, 162–64; Howard R. Lamar, *The Far Southwest, 1846–1912: A Territorial History*, rev. ed. (Albuquerque: University of New Mexico Press, 2000), 378–79; Richard White, *Railroaded: The Transcontinentals and the Making of Modern America* (New York: W. W. Norton, 2011), 25.

15. Ronald Walters, *American Reformers, 1815–1860* (New York: Hill & Wang, 1997); Eric Foner, *Reconstruction: America's Unfinished Revolution, 1863–1877* (New York: Harper & Row, 1988). On Republicans as conservatives, see Adam I. P. Smith, *Stormy Present: Conservatism and the Problem of Slavery in Northern Politics, 1846–1865* (Chapel Hill: University of North Carolina Press, 2017); as reformers, James Oakes, *Freedom National: The Destruction of Slavery in the United States, 1861–1865* (New York: W. W. Norton, 2012).

16. Nichols, *Lincoln and the Indians*, 129–31; Lincoln to Williamson Durley, Springfield, October 3, 1845, *Collected Works*, 1:347–48; October 28, 1863, in Tyler Dennett, ed., *Lincoln and the Civil War in the Diaries and Letters of John Hay* (New York: Dodd, Mead, 1939), 108; Hans L.

Trefousse, *The Radical Republicans: Lincoln's Vanguard for Racial Justice, 1863–1869* (New York: Alfred A. Knopf, 1969).

17. Lincoln, "Annual Message to Congress," December 3, 1861, *Collected Works*, 5:35–54, at 46; Office of Indian Affairs, *Annual Report of the Commissioner of Indian Affairs, for the Year 1861* (Washington, DC: Government Printing Office, 1862), 4.

18. Office of Indian Affairs, *Annual Report of the Commissioner of Indian Affairs, for the Year 1861*, 5.

19. Ibid., 17.

20. Office of Indian Affairs, *Annual Report of the Commissioner of Indian Affairs, for the Year 1862*, 28, 11.

21. *Report of the Commissioner of Indian Affairs, for the Year 1863* (Washington, DC: Government Printing Office, 1864), 5–7.

22. *Report of the Commissioner of Indian Affairs, for the Year 1864* (Washington, DC: Government Printing Office, 1865), 3–8.

23. *The New York Times*, January 31, 1863.

24. *The New York Times*, June 27, 1863, and August 16, 1863; Danziger, *Indians and Bureaucrats*, 68–69.

25. Nichols, *Lincoln and the Indians*, 132–33; Gustav Niebuhr, *Lincoln's Bishop: A President, a Priest, and the Fate of 300 Dakota Sioux Warriors* (New York: HarperOne, 2014), 5–14.

26. Nichols, *Lincoln and the Indians*, 133–35; Niebuhr, *Lincoln's Bishop*, 121–26; Lincoln to Henry B. Whipple, Washington, March 27, 1862, *Collected Works*, 5:173.

27. Nichols, *Lincoln and the Indians*, 135–36; Niebuhr, *Lincoln's Bishop*, 126.

28. Niebuhr, *Lincoln's Bishop*, 1–4, 126–31; Salmon P. Chase to Lincoln, n.d. [1862], Abraham Lincoln Papers, Series 1, General Correspondence, 1833–1916, Library of Congress.

29. Nichols, *Lincoln and the Indians*, 139–41; Niebuhr, *Lincoln's Bishop*, 131–33.

30. Nichols, *Lincoln and the Indians*, 146; Lincoln, "Annual Message to Congress," December 1, 1862, *Collected Works*, 5:526; Niebuhr, *Lincoln's Bishop*, 132–35.

31. Nichols, *Lincoln and the Indians*, 144–57.

32. Lincoln, "Annual Message to Congress," December 8, 1863, *Collected Works*, 7:47–48.

33. Lincoln to William Windom, Washington, March 30, 1864, Abraham Lincoln Papers, Series 3, General Correspondence, 1837–1897, Library of Congress; Lincoln, "Annual Message to Congress," December 6, 1864, *Collected Works*, 8:146–47; Nichols, *Lincoln and the Indians*, 157–59.

34. William L. Lang, "John Beeson (1803–1889)," *Oregon Encyclopedia*, https://web.archive.org/web/20180521020517/https://oregonencyclopedia.org/articles/beeson_john_1803_1889_/; Nichols, *Lincoln and the Indians*, 130.

35. Nichols, *Lincoln and the Indians*, 130, 142–43, 158, 200–01; C. Joseph Gentin-Pilawa, *Crooked Paths to Allotment: The Fight over Federal Indian Policy after the Civil War* (Chapel Hill: University of North Carolina Press, 2012), 53–54; Henry E. Fritz, *The Movement for Indian Assimilation, 1860–1890* (Philadelphia: University of Pennsylvania Press, 1963), 37.

36. Fritz, *Movement for Indian Assimilation*, 40–41, 45; Danziger, *Indians and Bureaucrats*, 11.

37. Nichols, *Lincoln and the Indians*, 140, 147–60.

38. David W. Blight, *Frederick Douglass: Prophet of Freedom* (New York: Simon & Schuster, 2018), 7; "Oration in Memory of Abraham Lincoln, Delivered at the Unveiling of the Freedmen's Monument in Memory of Abraham Lincoln in Lincoln Park, Washington, D.C., April 14, 1876," in Philip S. Foner, ed., *The Life and Writings of Frederick Douglass*, 4 vols. (New York: International, 1955), 4, 312–16; Frederick Douglass, *Life and Times of Frederick Douglass, Written by Himself* (Hartford, CT: Park, 1882), 422; Lincoln, "First Debate with Stephen A. Douglas at Ottawa, Illinois," August 21, 1858, *Collected Works*, 3:16.

39. Wolfgang Mieder, "'The Only Good Indian Is a Dead Indian': History and Meaning of a Proverbial Stereotype," *Journal of American Folklore* 106, no. 419 (Winter 1993): 38–60, esp. 44–45.

40. Lincoln, *Washington Daily Morning Chronicle*, March 28, 1863, *Collected Works*, 6:151–53. The other quotations come from this source, except the final one, which is from Mary Jane Warde, *When the Wolf Came: The Civil War and Indian Territory* (Fayetteville: University of Arkansas Press, 2013), 226.

41. Nichols, *Lincoln and the Indians*, 186–87.

42. Dole to Lincoln, Washington, July 8, 1864, Abraham Lincoln Papers, Series 1, Correspondence, 1833–1916, Library of Congress; The Lincoln Log, Lincoln Sesquicentennial Commission, http://www.thelincolnlog .org/Results.aspx?type=CalendarDay&day=1864-07-08 (see the link there to "Proclamation concerning Reconstruction," *Collected Works*, 7:43–44).

## 4. The Problem with Indian Territory

1. Brad Agnew, "Our Doom as a Nation Is Sealed: The Five Nations in the Civil War," in Bradley R. Clampitt, ed., *The Civil War and Reconstruction in Indian Territory* (Lincoln: University of Nebraska Press, 2015), 67–68; Charles H. Davis, "William Gaston Coffin and His Wabash & Erie Canal Connections Revisited," *Hoosier Packet*, May 2015; Mary Jane Warde, *When the Wolf Came: The Civil War and the Indian Territory* (Fayetteville: University of Arkansas Press, 2013).

2. Nichols, *Lincoln and the Indians*, 34–39.

3. Clampitt, *Indian Territory*, 1–15; Danziger, *Indians and Bureaucrats*, 167; Christopher Phillips, *The Rivers Ran Backward: The Civil War and the Remaking of the American Middle Border* (New York: Oxford University Press, 2016).

4. Nichols, *Lincoln and the Indians*, 25–31; Robert M. Utley, *The Indian Frontier of the American West, 1846–1890* (Albuquerque: University of New Mexico Press, 1984), 72–73; Danziger, *Indians and Bureaucrats*, 168.

5. Clampitt, *Indian Territory*, 6–7; Richard B. McCaslin, "Bitter Legacy: The Battle Front," in ibid., 20; Nichols, *Lincoln and the Indians*, 29–32; Utley, *Indian Frontier*, 73; Clarissa W. Confer, *The Cherokee Nation in the Civil War* (Norman: University of Oklahoma Press, 2012); Troy Smith, "Nations Colliding: The Civil War Comes to Indian Territory," *Civil War History* 59, no. 3 (September 2013): 279–319, at 285–87.

6. *New York Tribune*, June 20, 1861; Agnew, "Our Doom," 68–70; Utley, *Indian Frontier*, 73; Warde, *When the Wolf Came*, 41; Gary E. Moulton, *John Ross: Cherokee Chief* (Athens: University of Georgia Press, 1978); Kenny Arthur Franks, *Stand Watie and the Agony of the Cherokee Nation* (Memphis: Memphis State University Press, 1979).

7. Kent Blansett, "When the Stars Fell from the Sky: The Cherokee Nation and Autonomy in the Civil War," in Virginia Scharff, ed., *Empire and Liberty: The Civil War and the West* (Oakland: Autry National Center for the American West and University of California Press, 2015), 96; Annie H. Abel, *The American Indian in the Civil War, 1862–1865*, repr. (Lincoln: University of Nebraska Press, 1992), 85.

8. D. Cooper to Simon Cameron, St. Paul, Minnesota, May 1, 1861, *Official Records of the War of Rebellion*, Series 3, vol. 1 (Washington, DC: Government Printing Office, 1880–1910), 140; Cameron to Cooper, Washington, May 9, 1861, in ibid., 184; *New York Tribune*, October 9, 1861; David Hunter to Lorenzo Thomas, Fort Leavenworth, November 27, 1861, Abraham Lincoln Papers, Series 1, General Correspondence, 1833–1916, Library of Congress; Nichols, *Lincoln and the Indians*, 39–41.

9. Lincoln, "Annual Message to Congress," December 3, 1861, *Collected Works*, 5:46.

10. United States Office of Indian Affairs, *Annual Report of the Commissioner of Indian Affairs, for the Year 1861* (Washington, DC: Government Printing Office, 1861), 3–4.

11. John David Smith, *Lincoln and the U.S. Colored Troops* (Carbondale: Southern Illinois University Press, 2013).

12. *The New York Times*, July 4, 1866; Ian Michael Spurgeon, *Man of Douglas, Man of Lincoln: The Political Odyssey of James Henry Lane* (Columbia: University of Missouri Press, 2008); Edward A. Miller Jr., *Lincoln's Abolitionist General: A Biography of David Hunter* (Columbia: University of South Carolina Press, 1997).

13. William G. Coffin and Mark Delahay to Lincoln, Washington, October 21, 1861, Abraham Lincoln Papers, Library of Congress, Series 1, General Correspondence, 1833–1916, at https://www.loc.gov/resource/mal.1257300/?sp=1&st=text&r=0.151,0.006,1.207,0.99,0; Nichols, *Lincoln and the Indians*, 36.

14. Lincoln to Cameron, Washington, December 16, 1861, *Collected Works*, 5:71.

15. Lincoln to Hunter, Washington, October 24, 1861, *Collected Works*, 5:1–2; Nichols, *Lincoln and the Indians*, 35.

16. Hunter to Lincoln, Fort Leavenworth, December 23, 1861, Abraham Lincoln Papers, Series 1, Correspondence, 1833–1916, Library of Congress.

17. Lincoln to Hunter, Washington, December 31, 1861, *Collected Works*, 5:84–85.

18. Nichols, *Lincoln and the Indians*, 40–43.

19. Delahay to Lincoln, Leavenworth, January 28, 1862, Abraham Lincoln Papers, Library of Congress, Series 1, General Correspondence, 1833–1916, at https://www.loc.gov/item/mal1419700/; Lincoln to Edwin Stanton, Washington, January 31, 1862, *Collected Works*, 5:115–16; Nichols, *Lincoln and the Indians*, 46.

20. Dole to Lincoln, Washington, February 3, 1862, Abraham Lincoln Papers, Library of Congress, Series 1, General Correspondence, 1833–1916; Hunter to Lincoln, Kansas, February 14, 1862, ibid.

21. Lincoln to Hunter, Washington, February 10, 1862, *Collected Works*, 5:132. The *Official Records* lists the letter as being to Hunter and Lane.

22. Nichols, *Lincoln and the Indians*, 47–49; Utley, *Indian Frontier*, 75; McCaslin, "Bitter Legacy," 23–24; Blansett, "When the Stars Fell," 95.

23. Nichols, *Lincoln and the Indians*, 49–50, 61.

24. Ibid., 50–52; Agnew, "Our Doom," 72–73.

25. Agnew, "Our Doom," 73–74; Office of Indian Affairs, *Annual Report of the Commissioner of Indian Affairs, for the Year 1862* (Washington, DC: Government Printing Office, 1862), 3.

26. James G. Blunt to Lincoln, In the Field, Fort Scott, August 13, 1862, Abraham Lincoln Papers, Series 1, General Correspondence, 1833–1916, Library of Congress.

27. Delahay to Lincoln, Leavenworth City, August 21, 1862, in ibid.

28. Lincoln to Smith, Washington, September 11, 1862, *Collected Works*, 5:415–16; Nichols, *Lincoln and the Indians*, 55–57.

29. John Ross to Lincoln, Lawrenceville, New Jersey, September 16, 1862, Abraham Lincoln Papers, Series 1, General Correspondence, 1833–1916, Library of Congress.

30. Lincoln to Ross, Washington, September 25, 1862, in ibid.

31. Smith to Lincoln, Washington, September 29, 1862, in ibid.; Nichols, *Lincoln and the Indians*, 56; Lincoln to Samuel Curtis, Washington, October 10, 1862, *Collected Works*, 5:456.

32. Lincoln, "Annual Message to Congress," December 1, 1862, *Collected Works*, 5:518–37, at 525.

33. Linda W. Reese, "'We Had a Lot of Trouble Getting Things Settled after the War': The Freedpeople's Civil Wars," in Clampitt, *Indian Territory*, 136–37; Agnew, "Our Doom," 74–75.

34. Lincoln, "Proclamation of Amnesty and Reconstruction," December 8, 1863, *Collected Works*, 7:53–56; Curtis to Colonel William A. Phillips, February 11, 1864, *Official Records*, Series 1, vol. 34, part 2, 301–02; Agnew, "Our Doom," 76.

35. Curtis to Lincoln, Fort Leavenworth, February 28, 1864, Abraham Lincoln Papers, Series 1, Correspondence, 1833–1916, Library of Congress.

36. Lincoln to Stanton, Washington, January 9, 1864, *Collected Works*, 7:119; Lincoln to the Senate, Washington, May 14, 1864, in ibid., 7:341.

37. Lincoln to the Senate, Washington, May 14, 1864, in ibid., 7:341; Nichols, *Lincoln and the Indians*, 62–64; Agnew, "Our Doom," 76–77; Warde, *When the Wolf Came*, 242–43; Danziger, *Indians and Bureaucrats*, 176–77.

38. Agnew, "Our Doom," 78–80; Christopher Bean, "Who Defines a Nation? Reconstruction in Indian Territory," in Clampitt, *Indian Territory*, 111–15.

39. Smith, "Indian Territory," 316–19; Clampitt, *Indian Territory*.

## 5. Lincoln and the Dakota

1. Etulain, *Lincoln Looks West*, 29–30; Richard Striner, *Lincoln and Race* (Carbondale: Southern Illinois University Press, 2010), 65. See especially works by Gary Clayton Anderson, most recently *Massacre in Minnesota: The Dakota War of 1862, the Most Violent Ethnic Conflict in American History* (Norman: University of Oklahoma Press, 2019), which I have relied on heavily for details in this chapter.

2. Scott W. Berg, *38 Nooses: Lincoln, Little Crow, and the Beginning of the Frontier's End* (New York: Pantheon Books, 2012), 10–11; Nichols, *Lincoln and the Indians*, 76; Danziger, *Indians and Bureaucrats*, 95–99; Anderson, *Massacre in Minnesota*, 17–72.

3. Martin Ridge, *Ignatius Donnelly: The Portrait of a Politician* (Chicago: University of Chicago Press, 1962), 66–67; Danziger, *Indians and Bureaucrats*, 99–04.

4. Berg, *38 Nooses*, 28–29; Ridge, *Ignatius Donnelly*, 66–67; Utley, *Indian Frontier*, 76; Anderson, *Massacre in Minnesota*, 77–79.

5. Utley, *Indian Frontier*, 78.

6. Berg, *38 Nooses*, 37–38; Nichols, *Lincoln and the Indians*, 66–67; Anderson, *Massacre in Minnesota*, 73.

7. Nichols, *Lincoln and the Indians*, 68–70.

8. George E. H. Day to Lincoln, St. Anthony, Minnesota, January 1, 1862, Abraham Lincoln Papers, Series 1, General Correspondence, 1833–1916, Library of Congress; Nichols, *Lincoln and the Indians*, 70–75.

9. Nichols, *Lincoln and the Indians*, 132.

10. Ibid., 77; Anderson, *Massacre in Minnesota*, 82. This section relies for details on Nichols, *Lincoln and the Indians*, 65–118; Anderson, *Massacre in Minnesota*, 84–111; Berg, *38 Nooses*; Paul N. Beck, *Columns of Vengeance: Soldiers, Sioux, and the Punitive Expeditions, 1863–1864* (Norman: University of Oklahoma Press, 2013), 25–49; and Dole's account in Office of Indian Affairs, *Annual Report of the Commissioner of Indian Affairs, for the Year 1862* (Washington, DC: Government Printing Office, 1862), 12–21.

11. H. H. Sibley to Ramsey, Headquarters, Indian Expedition, August 20, 1862, *Minnesota in the Civil and Indian Wars*, 2 vols. (St. Paul: Pioneer Press, 1890–93), 2:165; Sibley to Ramsey, St. Peter, August 24, 1862, in ibid., 198. Ibid., 165–93, includes the various reports. See also Anderson, *Massacre in Minnesota*, 135–60.

12. Ramsey to Stanton, St. Paul, August 21, 1862, *Official Records*, 1:13, 590; Ramsey to Stanton, St. Paul, August 21, 1862, *Minnesota in the Civil and Indian Wars*, 194–95; Ramsey to Stanton, Minneapolis, August 22, 1862, *Official Records*, 2:4, 417.

13. Henry W. Halleck to Ramsey, War Department, August 24, 1862, and Halleck to John Schofield, *Minnesota in the Civil and Indian Wars*, 2:196; Halleck to Ramsey, War Department, August 25, 1862, in ibid., 199; Ramsey to Halleck, St. Paul, August 26, 1862, in ibid., 200; Halleck to Ramsey, August 29, 1862, in ibid., 209; David Tod to Stanton, Columbus, September 9, 1862, *Official Records*, 2:4, 499; Stanton to Tod, Washington, September 9, 1862, in ibid. On Harney and the Lakota, see Paul N. Beck, *The First Sioux War: The Grattan Fight and Blue Water Creek, 1854–1856* (Lanham, MD: University Press of America, 2004), esp. 124–25.

14. John Hay to John G. Nicolay, Washington, August 11, 1862, in Michael Burlingame, ed., *At Lincoln's Side: John Hay's Civil War Correspondence and Selected Writings* (Carbondale: Southern Illinois University Press, 2000), 24; Zeitz, *Lincoln's Boys*, 127–29.

15. Zeitz, *Lincoln's Boys*, 127–29; Berg, *38 Nooses*, 117; Burlingame, *With Lincoln in the White House*, 88; Mark Diedrich, "Chief Hole-in-the-Day and the 1862 Chippewa Disturbance: A Reappraisal," *Minnesota History Magazine* 50, no. 5 (Spring 1987): 193–203.

16. Ramsey to Stanton, St. Paul, August 25, 1862, in *Minnesota in the Civil and Indian Wars*, 2:199; Ramsey to Lincoln, St. Paul, August 26, 1862,

in ibid., 200; Morton S. Wilkinson, William P. Dole, and John G. Nicolay to Lincoln, St. Paul, August 27, 1862, in ibid., 201.

17. Nicolay to Stanton, St. Paul, August 27, 1862, *Official Records*, 1:13, 599–600.

18. Lincoln to Ramsey, Executive Mansion, August 27, 1862, *Minnesota in the Civil and Indian Wars*, 2:201; Ramsey to Lincoln, St. Paul, September 6, 1862, in ibid., 224–25; Nichols, *Lincoln and the Indians*, 84; Joseph L. Williams, Walter A. Burleigh, and William Jayne to Lincoln, Greenwood, December 27, 1862, Abraham Lincoln Papers, Series 1, Correspondence, 1833–1916, Library of Congress; Richard N. Ellis, *General Pope and U.S. Indian Policy* (Albuquerque: University of New Mexico Press, 1970), 5.

19. Stanton to Pope, Washington, September 6, 1862, *Minnesota in the Civil and Indian Wars*, 2:225.

20. *The New York Times*, July 15, 1862.

21. Pope to Halleck, St. Paul, September 16, 1862, *Minnesota in the Civil and Indian Wars*, 2:232; Pope to Sibley, St. Paul, September 17, 1862, in ibid., 233–34; Pope to Stanton, St. Paul, September 22, 1862, in ibid., 237–38.

22. Lincoln to Stanton, Executive Mansion, September 20, 1862, *Collected Works*, 5:432; Pope to Halleck, St. Paul, September 23, 1862, *Minnesota in the Civil and Indian Wars*, 2:238–39; Pope to Stanton, St. Paul, September 25, 1862, in ibid., 251; Halleck to Pope, Washington, September 25, 1862, in ibid., 252; Pope to Halleck, St. Paul, October 4, 1862, in ibid., 264; Berg, *38 Nooses*, 170–71, 186–87.

23. Pope to Sibley, St. Paul, September 28, 1862, *Minnesota in the Civil and Indian Wars*, 2:257.

24. Pope to Halleck, St. Paul, October 2, 1862, in ibid., 260; Halleck to Pope, Washington, October 3, 1862, in ibid., 261; Pope to Halleck, St. Paul, October 7, 1862, in ibid., 266; Ramsey to Stanton, St. Paul, October 15, 1862, in ibid., 277; Halleck to Pope, Washington, October 28, 1862, in ibid., 284.

25. Benjamin Wade to Lincoln, September 30, 1862, *Collected Works*, 5:455; Lincoln to Stanton, Washington, October 9, 1862, in ibid.

26. Pope to Halleck, St. Paul, October 9, *Minnesota in the Civil and Indian Wars*, 2:270; October 10, in ibid., 272; October 13, in ibid., 274.

27. William E. Gienapp and Erica L. Gienapp, eds., *The Civil War Diary of Gideon Welles: Lincoln's Secretary of the Navy* (Urbana: University of Illinois Press, 2014), 77; Stanton to Pope, Washington, October 14, 1862, *Minnesota in the Civil and Indian Wars*, 2:276.

28. Ramsey to Lincoln, St. Paul, October 22, 1862, *Minnesota in the Civil and Indian Wars*, 2:282–83; Richard Chute to Ramsey, Washington,

November 5, 1862, in ibid., 286–87; Wilkinson to Ramsey, Washington, December 9, 1862, in ibid., 292.

29. Pope to Ramsey, St. Paul, November 6, 1862, in ibid., 2:287–88; Nichols, *Lincoln and the Indians*, 155–57.

30. Ramsey to Lincoln, St. Paul, November 10, 1862, *Official Records*, 1:xiii, 787.

31. Lincoln to Pope, Washington, November 10, 1862; Pope to Lincoln, St. Paul, November 11, 1862; Ramsey to Lincoln, St. Paul, November 10, 1862; and Pope to Lincoln, St. Paul, November 24, 1862, all in *Minnesota in the Civil and Indian Wars*, 2:289–90. See also Ramsey to Lincoln, November 10, 1862, *Official Records*, 1:xiii, 787; Pope to Lincoln, November 11, 1862, in ibid., 788; Lincoln to Pope, Executive Mansion, November 10, 1862, *Collected Works*, 5:493; Ramsey to Lincoln, St. Paul, November 28, 1862, Abraham Lincoln Papers, Series 1, Correspondence, 1833–1916, Library of Congress.

32. Danziger, *Indians and Bureaucrats*, 106–09; *The New York Times*, November 29, 1862.

33. Dole to Caleb B. Smith, Washington, November 10, 1862, Abraham Lincoln Papers, Series 1, Correspondence, 1833–1916, Library of Congress; Smith to Lincoln, Washington, November 11, 1862, in ibid.; Anderson, *Massacre in Minnesota*, 245–46.

34. Thaddeus Williams to Lincoln, St. Paul, November 22, 1862, Abraham Lincoln Papers, Series 1, Correspondence, 1833–1916, Library of Congress; Stephen Riggs to Lincoln, St. Anthony, November 17, 1862, in ibid.

35. Henry M. Rice to Lincoln, Washington, November 20, 1862, in ibid.; Berg, *38 Nooses*, 210–11; Niebuhr, *Lincoln's Bishop*, 136–40.

36. Lincoln, "Annual Message to Congress," December 1, 1862, *Collected Works*, 5:525–26.

37. Ibid., 525–26, 540–41.

38. Ibid.; Office of Indian Affairs, *Annual Report of the Commissioner of Indian Affairs, for the Year 1862* (Washington, DC: Government Printing Office, 1862), 6–7.

39. Lincoln to Joseph Holt, Washington, December 1, 1862, *Collected Works*, 5:537–38; Holt to Lincoln, Washington, December 1, 1862, Abraham Lincoln Papers, Series 1, Correspondence, 1833–1916, Library of Congress; Nichols, *Lincoln and the Indians*, 99–101; Anderson, *Massacre in Minnesota*, 228.

40. Nichols, *Lincoln and the Indians*, 108.

41. Lincoln to Sibley, Washington, December 6, 1862, *Collected Works*, 542–43; Berg, *38 Nooses*, 219–21.

42. Wilkinson to Ramsey, Washington, December 9, 1862, *Minnesota in the Civil and Indian Wars*, 2:291.

43. Lincoln to Smith, Washington, December 5, 1862, *Collected Works*, 5:541; Lincoln, "To the Senate of the United States," December 11, 1862, in ibid., 5:550–51.

44. Lincoln to Smith, Washington, December 5, 1862, in ibid., 5:541; Lincoln, "To the Senate of the United States," December 11, 1862, in ibid., 5:550–51; Ron Soodalter, "The Quality of Mercy: Abraham Lincoln and the Presidential Power to Pardon," in Charles L. Hubbard, ed., *Lincoln, the Law, and Presidential Leadership* (Carbondale: Southern Illinois University Press, 2015), 126–27; Lincoln to Sibley, Washington, December 16, 1862, *Minnesota in the Civil and Indian Wars*, 2:292; Burlingame, *With Lincoln in the White House*, 94.

45. Soodalter, "Quality of Mercy," 126–27; Lincoln to Sibley, Washington, December 16, 1862, *Minnesota in the Civil and Indian Wars*, 2:292; Sibley to Lincoln, St. Paul, December 15, 1862, Abraham Lincoln Papers, Series 1, Correspondence, 1833–1916, Library of Congress.

46. *The New York Times*, December 12, 1862.

47. Sibley to Lincoln, St. Paul, December 27, 1862, and January 7 and February 16, 1863, Abraham Lincoln Papers, Series 1, General Correspondence, 1833–1916, Library of Congress; Soodalter, "Quality of Mercy," 126–27.

48. Office of Indian Affairs, *Annual Report of the Commissioner of Indian Affairs, for the Year 1863* (Washington, DC: Government Printing Office, 1863), 19; Ellis, *General Pope*, 31–51.

49. Lincoln to Galusha A. Grow, Washington, February 13, 1863, *Collected Works*, 6:104; House Executive Document no. 68, 37th Congress, 3rd Session, 3; Dole to Lincoln, Washington, April 28, 1862, and Lincoln, "Order for Pardon of Sioux Indians," April 30, 1864, *Collected Works*, 7:325–26; Nichols, *Lincoln and the Indians*, 120; Ramsey to Lincoln, St. Paul, May 22, 1863, Abraham Lincoln Papers, Series 1, General Correspondence, 1833–1916, Library of Congress.

50. Lincoln to Grow, Washington, February 13, 1863, *Collected Works*, 6:104; *Christian Recorder*, November 28, 1863; Message from the President of the United States, House Executive Documents nos. 1 and 68, 37th Congress, 3rd Session; *The New York Times*, October 12 and December 12, 1862; *New York Tribune*, August 25, 1862; Office of Indian Affairs, *Annual Report of the Commissioner of Indian Affairs, for the Year 1862*, 4–5; Berg, *38 Nooses*, 155–56.

51. Office of Indian Affairs, *Annual Report of the Commissioner of Indian Affairs, for the Year 1862*, 22; Danziger, *Indians and Bureaucrats*, 95–114; Niebuhr, *Lincoln's Bishop*, 164; Nichols, *Lincoln and the Indians*, 118.

52. Danziger, *Indians and Bureaucrats*, 95–114; Niebuhr, *Lincoln's Bishop*, 164; Nichols, *Lincoln and the Indians*, 118.

53. Office of Indian Affairs, *Annual Report of the Commissioner of Indian Affairs, for the Year 1863*, 31–32, 266–98.

54. Nichols, *Lincoln and the Indians*, 113–18.

55. John Fabian Witt, *Lincoln's Code: The Laws of War in American History* (New York: Free Press, 2012), esp. 330–33 and 184; Maeve Herbert, "Explaining the Sioux Military Commission of 1862," *Columbia Human Rights Law Review* 40, no. 3 (Spring 2009): 743–98; Burrus M. Carnahan, "Lincoln, Lieber, and the Laws of War: The Origins of the Principle of Military Necessity," *American Journal of International Law* 92, no. 2 (April 1998): 213–31.

56. Nichols, *Lincoln and the Indians*, 82–83; Berg, *38 Nooses*, 100–101; Stanley P. Hirshson, *The White Tecumseh: A Biography of General William T. Sherman* (New York: Wiley, 1998).

## 6. Peopling and Unpeopling the West

1. Richard W. Etulain, "Abraham Lincoln and the Trans-Mississippi American West: An Introductory Overview," in Etulain, *Lincoln Looks West*, 1; Durwood Ball, "Liberty, Empire, and Civil War," in Virginia Scharff, ed., *Empire and Liberty: The Civil War and the West* (Oakland: Autry National Center for the American West and University of California Press, 2015), 68–69; Carlos A. Schwantes, *In Mountain Shadows: A History of Idaho* (Lincoln: University of Nebraska Press, 1991), 47; Danziger, *Indians and Bureaucrats*, 50, 74; Megan Kate Nelson, *The Three-Cornered War: The Union, the Confederacy, and Native Peoples in the Fight for the West* (New York: Scribner, 2020).

2. Burlingame, *Lincoln*, 2:809. On veterans in the West, see William Deverell, "Redemption Falls Short: Soldier and Surgeon in the Post-Civil War Far West," in Adam Arenson and Andrew R. Graybill, eds., *Civil War Wests: Testing the Limits of the United States* (Oakland: University of California Press, 2015), 139–57.

3. Nichols, *Lincoln and the Indians*, 195.

4. Diane Mutti Burke, "Scattered People: The Long History of Forced Eviction in the Kansas-Missouri Borderlands," in Arenson and Graybill, *Civil War Wests*, 71–92; Nichols, *Lincoln and the Indians*, 195, 163.

5. Heather Cox Richardson, *"The Greatest Nation of the Earth": Republican Economic Policy during the Civil War* (Cambridge, MA: Harvard University Press, 1997), 5 and passim; Kevin Waite, "Jefferson Davis and Proslavery Visions of Empire in the Far West," *Journal of the Civil War Era* 6, no. 4 (December 2016): 536–65; Joseph A. Fry, *Dixie Looks Abroad: The South and U.S. Foreign Relations, 1789–1973* (Baton Rouge: Louisiana State University Press, 2002), 40–105.

6. Lincoln, "Annual Message to Congress," December 1, 1862, *Collected Works*, 5:518–37; Lincoln, "Annual Message to Congress," December 6,

1864, in ibid., 8:145–46; Nichols, *Lincoln and the Indians*, 164; Robert W. Johannsen, "The Tribe of Abraham: Lincoln and the Washington Territory," in Etulain, *Lincoln Looks West*, 153–73, at 165; Richardson, *Greatest Nation*, 170–208; Robert Lee et al., "Land-Grab Universities: Expropriated Indigenous Land Is the Foundation of the Land Grant University System," *High Country News* 52, no. 4 (April 2020): 32–45.

7. Ball, "Liberty, Empire, and Civil War," 68–69; Edmund S. Morgan, *American Slavery, American Freedom: The Ordeal of Colonial Virginia* (New York: W. W. Norton, 1975).

8. Benjamin Madley, *An American Genocide: The United States and the California Indian Catastrophe, 1846–1873* (New Haven, CT: Yale University Press, 2009); Brendan C. Lindsay, *Murder State: California's Native American Genocide, 1846–1873* (Lincoln: University of Nebraska Press, 2012); Richardson, *Greatest Nation*, 175; *San Francisco Daily Evening Bulletin*, July 15, 1861.

9. Hauptmann, *Between Two Fires*, 9; Nichols, *Lincoln and the Indians*, 162; *San Francisco Daily Evening Bulletin*, June 20, 1861.

10. Nichols, *Lincoln and the Indians*, 162; *Congressional Globe*, 38th Congress, 1st Session, March 18, 1864, 1209; Danziger, *Indians and Bureaucrats*, 190–92.

11. Danziger, *Indians and Bureaucrats*, 150–62; Benjamin Madley, "Understanding Genocide in California under United States Rule, 1846–1873," *Western Historical Quarterly* 47, no. 4 (Winter 2016): 449–61; Benjamin Madley, "'Unholy Traffic in Human Blood and Souls': Systems of California Indian Servitude under U.S. Rule," *Pacific Historical Review* 83, no. 4 (November 2014): 626–67.

12. Ralph J. Roske, *Everyman's Eden: A History of California* (New York: Macmillan, 1968), 348–49; Alvin M. Josephy, *The Civil War in the American West* (New York: Alfred A. Knopf, 1991), 240–44.

13. Ned Blackhawk, *Violence over the Land: Indians and Empires in the Early American West* (Cambridge, MA: Harvard University Press, 2006), 255–57; E. B. Long, *The Saints and the Union: Utah Territory during the Civil War* (Urbana: University of Illinois Press, 1981); John Gary Maxwell, *The Civil War Years in Utah: The Kingdom of God and the Territory That Did Not Fight* (Norman: University of Oklahoma Press, 2016); W. Paul Reeve, *Making Space on the Western Frontier: Mormons, Miners, and Southern Paiutes* (Urbana: University of Illinois Press, 2006). The Stephen Harding papers at Lilly Library, Indiana University, teem with his warnings of conspiracies.

14. Howard R. Lamar, *The Far Southwest, 1846–1912: A Territorial History*, rev. ed. (Albuquerque: University of New Mexico Press, 2000), 312; Danziger, *Indians and Bureaucrats*, 62–63; Blackhawk, *Violence over the Land*, 267–70.

15. *New York Tribune*, September 21, 1861; Lincoln to Caleb Smith, Washington, October 3, 1861, *Collected Works*, 4:548; Danziger, *Indians and Bureaucrats*, 62–63; Blackhawk, *Violence over the Land*, 259–62. Lincoln, "To the Senate of the United States," Washington, January 7, 1864, *Collected Works*, 7:112–13, lists several treaties involving Doty.

16. William P. Dole, *Report of the Commissioner of Indian Affairs*, November 26, 1862 (Washington, DC: Government Printing Office, 1862), 185–86; Lamar, *Far Southwest*, 312; Long, *Saints and the Union*, 104–30.

17. Long, *Saints and the Union*, 130, 141; Maxwell, *Civil War Years*, 190–92; Blackhawk, *Violence over the Land*, 263; Schwantes, *In Mountain Shadows*, 72.

18. Brigham Madsen, *Glory Hunter: A Biography of Patrick Edward Connor* (Salt Lake City: University of Utah Press, 1990), 79; *The New York Times*, February 25, 1863; *New York Tribune*, April 1, 1863.

19. *The New York Times*, April 26, 1863; Eugene P. Moehring, *Urbanism and Empire in the Far West, 1840–1890* (Reno: University of Nevada Press, 2004), 114.

20. *The New York Times*, October 12, 1862; Lamar, *Far Southwest*, 312; Steven J. Crum, *The Road on Which We Came: A History of the Western Shoshone* (Salt Lake City: University of Utah Press, 1994), 21–24; Robert W. Ellison, *Long Beard: Warren Wasson, Nevada's Pioneer Indian Agent, U.S. Marshal, Inventor, and Enigma* (Minden, NV: Hot Springs Mountain Press, 2008), 20–41.

21. Patrick E. Connor to Edward McGarry, Fort Ruby, September 29, 1862, *Official Records*, Series 1, vol. 50, part 2, 144; Crum, *The Road*, 23; Ellison, *Wasson*, 51–78; Long, *Saints and the Union*, 128.

22. Crum, *The Road*, 24–26; Jack D. Forbes, ed., *Nevada Indians Speak* (Reno: University of Nevada Press, 1967), 80–85.

23. Crum, *The Road*, 25–27; Blackhawk, *Violence over the Land*, 267–68.

24. Blackhawk, *Violence over the Land*, 267–70.

25. Danziger, *Indians and Bureaucrats*, 48.

26. Ibid., 28–29.

27. Thomas L. Karnes, *William Gilpin: Western Nationalist* (Austin: University of Texas Press, 1970), 253–98.

28. Nichols, *Lincoln and the Indians*, 197; Ari Kelman, *A Misplaced Massacre: Struggling over the Memory of Sand Creek* (Cambridge, MA: Harvard University Press, 2015), 146; Lamar, *Far Southwest*, 219.

29. Danziger, *Indians and Bureaucrats*, 27–28, 64–65; Nichols, *Lincoln and the Indians*, 168–70; Elliott West, *The Contested Plains: Indians, Goldseekers, and the Rush to Colorado* (Lawrence: University Press of Kansas, 1996), 293–94.

30. William J. Convery, "John Chivington," in Paul Andrew Hutton and Durwood Ball, eds., *Soldiers West: Biographies from the Military Frontier*,

2nd ed. (Norman: University of Oklahoma Press, 2009), 155, 157; Nichols, *Lincoln and the Indians*, 168–70; Kelman, *Misplaced Massacre*, 66–68.

31. Kelman, *Misplaced Massacre*, 14–15, 66–68, 147–48; Convery, "John Chivington," 153–54, 157; West, *Contested Plains*, 293–97.

32. Kelman, *Misplaced Massacre*; Stan Hoig, *The Sand Creek Massacre* (Norman: University of Oklahoma Press, 1961), 145–62; West, *Contested Plains*, 303–8.

33. West, *Contested Plains*, 307–8.

34. Kelman, *Misplaced Massacre*, 9–12, 17–18.

35. Hoig, *Sand Creek*, 162–66; Kelman, *Misplaced Massacre*, 13–16.

36. United States Congress, House of Representatives, *Massacre of the Cheyenne Indians, Report on the Conduct of the War, 38th Cong., 2nd sess.* (Washington, DC: Government Printing Office, 1865), iv, 5–6.

37. Lamar, *Far Southwest*, 197, 223.

38. Nichols, *Lincoln and the Indians*, 171–74, 208–11.

39. Richard W. Etulain, "Abraham Lincoln and the Trans-Mississippi West," in Etulain, *Lincoln Looks West*, 32–33.

40. Nichols, *Lincoln and the Indians*, 197; Ball, "Liberty, Empire, and Civil War," 68.

41. Jerry Thompson, ed., *Civil War in the Southwest: Recollections of the Sibley Brigade* (College Station: Texas A&M University Press, 2001); Andrew E. Masich, *The Civil War in Arizona: The Story of the California Volunteers, 1861–1865* (Norman: University of Oklahoma Press, 2006).

42. Lance R. Blyth, "Kit Carson and the War for the Southwest: Separation and Survival along the Rio Grande, 1862–1868," in Arenson and Graybill, *Civil War Wests*, 55–57; Martha C. Knack, *Boundaries Between: The Southern Paiutes, 1775–1995* (Lincoln: University of Nebraska Press, 1996), 97.

43. Danziger, *Indians and Bureaucrats*, 54–55.

44. Nichols, *Lincoln and the Indians*, 165–68; Knack, *Boundaries Between*, 97; Adam Kane, "James H. Carleton," in Hutton and Ball, *Soldiers West*, 135–39; David Remley, *Kit Carson: The Life of an American Border Man* (Norman: University of Oklahoma Press, 2011), 219–20; Lamar, *Far Southwest*, 108, 380–95; *San Francisco Daily Evening Bulletin*, June 7, 1861; Danziger, *Indians and Bureaucrats*, 181; Nelson, *Three-Cornered War*, 166–67.

45. Blyth, "Carson and the War for the Southwest," 60; Lamar, *Far Southwest*, 108; *The New York Times*, March 29, 1864; Peter Iverson, *Diné: A History of the Navajos* (Albuquerque: University of New Mexico Press, 2002), 51; Remley, *Kit Carson*, 218–39.

46. *The New York Times*, April 9, 1864.

47. Iverson, *Diné*, 49–50, 55; Danziger, *Indians and Bureaucrats*, 76–87.

48. Nichols, *Lincoln and the Indians*, 165–68; Lamar, *Far Southwest*, 108–12.

49. Iverson, *Diné*, 8; Nichols, *Lincoln and the Indians*, 165–68; James R. Doolittle, *Condition of the Indian Tribes: Report of the Special Committee Appointed under Joint Resolution of March 3, 1865, with Appendix [Reports of the Committees of the Senate]* (Washington, DC: Government Printing Office, 1867), 355–56.

50. John L. Kessell, "General Sherman and the Navajo Treaty of 1868: A Basic and Expedient Misunderstanding," *Western Historical Quarterly* 12, no. 3 (July 1981): 251–72.

## Conclusion

1. Nichols, *Lincoln and the Indians*, 164; Sven Beckert, *Empire of Cotton: A Global History* (New York: Vintage Books, 2014); 353; Bean, "Reconstruction," 124–25. See Elliott West, "Reconstructing Race," *Western Historical Quarterly* 34, no. 1 (Spring 2003): 6–26; Heather Cox Richardson, *West from Appomattox: The Reconstruction of America after the Civil War* (New Haven, CT: Yale University Press, 2008).

2. Richardson, *West from Appomattox*, 75–77; Charles W. Royster, *The Destructive War: William Tecumseh Sherman, Stonewall Jackson, and the Americans* (New York: Alfred A. Knopf, 1991), 393–99; Hirshson, *White Tecumseh*, 330–62.

3. Bean, "Reconstruction," 125–26; Reese, "'We Had a Lot of Trouble Getting Things Settled after the War': The Freedpeople's Civil Wars," 136; Earl M. Maltz, "Rethinking the Racial Boundaries of Citizenship: Native Americans and People of Chinese Descent," in Paul Quigley, ed., *The Civil War and the Transformation of American Citizenship* (Baton Rouge: Louisiana State University Press, 2018), 64–88, see 65–70; Lamar, *Far Southwest*, 113–14; Stephen Kantrowitz, "White Supremacy, Settler Colonialism, and the Two Citizenships of the Fourteenth Amendment," *Journal of the Civil War Era* 10, no. 1 (March 2020): 39.

4. Charles W. Calhoun, *The Presidency of Ulysses S. Grant* (Lawrence: University Press of Kansas, 2017), 265; Bean, "Reconstruction," 119–20; Agnew, "Our Doom," 81; Joan Waugh, *U. S. Grant: American Hero, American Myth* (Chapel Hill: University of North Carolina Press, 2009), 232–35.

5. Richard R. Levine, "Indian Fighters and Indian Reformers: Grant's Indian Peace Policy and the Conservative Consensus," *Civil War History* 31, no. 4 (December 1985): 329–52; Mary Stockwell, *Interrupted Odyssey: Ulysses S. Grant and the American Indians* (Carbondale: Southern Illinois University Press, 2018).

6. Ferenc Morton Szasz and Margaret Connell Szasz, *Lincoln and Religion* (Carbondale: Southern Illinois University Press, 2014), 37–38; Bean, "Reconstruction," 120; Nichols, *Lincoln and the Indians*, 159–60.

7. Bean, "Reconstruction," 125; Hans L. Trefousse, *Carl Schurz: A Biography* (Knoxville: University of Tennessee Press, 1982), 242–47.

8. William W. Freehling, *Becoming Lincoln* (Charlottesville: University of Virginia Press, 2018), 148; Allen C. Guelzo, *Lincoln and Douglas: The Debates That Defined America* (New York: Simon & Schuster, 2008), 191.

9. Nichols, *Lincoln and the Indians*, 199; Richard W. Etulain, "Abraham Lincoln and the Trans-Mississippi American West: An Introductory Overview," in Etulain, *Lincoln Looks West*, 32–33.

10. Heather Cox Richardson, *How the South Won the Civil War: Oligarchy, Democracy, and the Continuing Fight for the Soul of America* (New York: Oxford University Press, 2020); Eric Foner, *Reconstruction: America's Unfinished Revolution, 1863–1877* (New York: Harper & Row, 1988), 612.

# BIBLIOGRAPHY

## Books

Abel, Annie H. *The American Indian in the Civil War, 1862–1865*. Reprint, Lincoln: University of Nebraska Press, 1992.

———. *The Slaveholding Indians*. 3 vols. Cleveland: Arthur H. Clark, 1915–1925.

Allen, David Grayson. *In English Ways: The Movement of Societies and the Transferal of English Local Law and Custom to Massachusetts Bay in the Seventeenth Century*. New York: W. W. Norton, 1982.

Anderson, Gary Clayton. *Ethnic Cleansing and the Indian: The Crime That Should Haunt America*. Norman: University of Oklahoma Press, 2014.

———. *Massacre in Minnesota: The Dakota War of 1862, the Most Violent Ethnic Conflict in American History*. Norman: University of Oklahoma Press, 2019.

Arenson, Adam, and Andrew R. Graybill, eds. *Civil War Wests: Testing the Limits of the United States*. Oakland: University of California Press, 2015.

Armstrong, William H. *Warrior in Two Camps: Ely S. Parker, Union General and Seneca Chief*. Syracuse: Syracuse University Press, 1978.

Bailey, M. Thomas. *Reconstruction in Indian Territory: A Story of Avarice, Discriminations, and Opportunism*. Port Washington, NY: Kennikat Press, 1972.

Baker, George E., ed. *The Works of William H. Seward*. 5 vols. Boston: Houghton Mifflin, 1853–84.

Baker, Jean Harvey. *Mary Todd Lincoln: A Biography*. New York: W. W. Norton, 1987.

Barnhart, John D., and Dorothy L. Riker. *Indiana to 1816: The Colonial Period*. Indianapolis: Indiana Historical Bureau and Indiana Historical Society, 1971.

Basler, Roy P., ed. *The Collected Works of Abraham Lincoln*. 9 vols. New Brunswick, NJ: Rutgers University Press, 1953–55.

Beck, Paul N. *Columns of Vengeance: Soldiers, Sioux, and the Punitive Expeditions of 1863–1864*. Norman: University of Oklahoma Press, 2013.

Beckert, Sven. *Empire of Cotton: A Global History*. New York: Vintage Books, 2014.

Berg, Scott W. *38 Nooses: Lincoln, Little Crow, and the Beginning of the Frontier's End*. New York: Pantheon Books, 2012.

Bingham, Caleb. *The American Preceptor; Being a New Selection of Lessons for Reading and Speaking. Designed for the Use of Schools*. Boston: Manning & Loring, 1811.

Blackhawk, Ned. *Violence over the Land: Indians and Empires in the Early American West*. Cambridge, MA: Harvard University Press, 2006.

Blair, Harry C., and Rebecca Tarshis. *Colonel Edward D. Baker: Lincoln's Constant Ally.* Portland: Oregon Historical Society, 1960.

Blight, David W. *Frederick Douglass: Prophet of Freedom.* New York: Simon & Schuster, 2018.

Blumenthal, Sidney. *A Self-Made Man: The Political Life of Abraham Lincoln.* Vol. 1. *1809–1849.* New York: Simon & Schuster, 2016.

———. *Wrestling with His Angel: The Political Life of Abraham Lincoln.* Vol. 2. *1849–1856.* New York: Simon & Schuster, 2017.

Borchard, Gregory A. *Lincoln and Horace Greeley.* Carbondale: Southern Illinois University Press, 2011.

Boritt, Gabor S. *Lincoln and the Economics of the American Dream.* Memphis: Memphis State University Press, 1978.

Boritt, Gabor S., and Norman O. Furness, eds. *The Historian's Lincoln: Pseudohistory, Psychohistory, and History.* Urbana: University of Illinois Press, 1988.

Bowes, John P. *Black Hawk and the War of 1832: Removal in the North.* New York: Chelsea House, 2007.

———. *Too Good for Indians: Northern Indian Removal.* Norman: University of Oklahoma Press, 2016.

Breen, T. H. *Puritans and Adventurers: Change and Persistence in Early America.* New York: Oxford University Press, 1980.

Brookhiser, Richard. *America's Dynasty: The Adamses.* New York: Free Press, 2002.

Brown, Dee. *Bury My Heart at Wounded Knee.* New York: Holt, Rinehart & Winston, 1971.

Brown, Thomas. *Politics and Statesmanship: Essays on the American Whig Party.* New York: Columbia University Press, 1985.

Burlingame, Michael. *Abraham Lincoln: A Life.* 2 vols. Baltimore: Johns Hopkins University Press, 2008.

———, ed. *At Lincoln's Side: John Hay's Civil War Correspondence and Selected Writings.* Carbondale: Southern Illinois University Press, 2000.

———, ed. *Lincoln's Journalist: John Hay's Anonymous Writings for the Press, 1860–1864.* Carbondale: Southern Illinois University Press, 1998.

———, ed. *An Oral History of Abraham Lincoln: John G. Nicolay's Interviews and Essays.* Carbondale: Southern Illinois University Press, 1996.

———, ed. *With Lincoln in the White House: Letters, Memoranda, and Other Writings of John G. Nicolay, 1860–1865.* Carbondale: Southern Illinois University Press, 2000.

Calhoun, Charles W. *The Presidency of Ulysses S. Grant.* Lawrence: University Press of Kansas, 2017.

Calloway, Colin G. *The Indian World of George Washington: The First President, the First Americans, and the Birth of the Nation.* New York: Oxford University Press, 2018.

Carman, Harry J., and Reinhard H. Luthin. *Lincoln and the Patronage*. New York: Columbia University Press, 1943.

Carwardine, Richard. *Lincoln's Sense of Humor*. Carbondale: Southern Illinois University Press, 2017.

Castel, Albert E. *A Frontier State at War: Kansas, 1861–1865*. Ithaca: Cornell University Press, 1958.

Cayton, Andrew R. L. *Frontier Indiana*. Bloomington: Indiana University Press, 1996.

Clampitt, Bradley R., ed. *The Civil War and Reconstruction in Indian Territory*. Lincoln: University of Nebraska Press, 2015.

Clinton, Catherine. *Mrs. Lincoln: A Life*. New York: HarperCollins, 2009.

Colton, Calvin, ed. *The Speeches of Henry Clay*. 2 vols. New York: A. S. Barnes, 1857.

Colton, Ray. *The Civil War in the Western Territories: Arizona, Colorado, New Mexico, and Utah*. Norman: University of Oklahoma Press, 1959.

Confer, Clarissa W. *The Cherokee Nation in the Civil War*. Norman: University of Oklahoma Press, 2012.

Cozzens, Peter. *General John Pope: A Life for the Nation*. Urbana: University of Illinois Press, 2000.

Cronon, William. *Changes in the Land: Indians, Colonists, and the Ecology of New England*. New York: Hill & Wang, 1983.

Crum, Steven J. *The Road on Which We Came: A History of the Western Shoshone*. Salt Lake City: University of Utah Press, 1994.

Cunliffe, Marcus L., ed. *The Life of Washington by Mason L. Weems*. Cambridge, MA: Harvard University Press, 1962.

Curry, Leonard P. *Blueprint for Modern America: Nonmilitary Legislation of the First Civil War Congress*. Nashville: Vanderbilt University Press, 1968.

Danizger, Edmund. *Indians and Bureaucrats: Administering the Reservation Policy during the Civil War*. Urbana: University of Illinois Press, 1974.

David, James Corbett. *Dunmore's New World: The Extraordinary Life of a Royal Governor in Revolutionary America—with Jacobites, Counterfeiters, Land Schemes, Shipwrecks, Scalping, Indian Politics, Runaway Slaves, and Two Illegal Royal Weddings*. Charlottesville: University of Virginia Press, 2013.

de Tocqueville, Alexis. *Democracy in America*. 2 vols. New York: Vintage Books, 1954. First published 1831.

Dennett, Tyler, ed. *Lincoln and the Civil War in the Diaries and Letters of John Hay*. New York: Dodd, Mead, 1939.

Dirck, Brian R. *Lincoln in Indiana*. Carbondale: Southern Illinois University Press, 2017.

Ellis, Richard N. *General Pope and U.S. Indian Policy*. Albuquerque: University of New Mexico Press, 1970.

Ellison, Robert W. *Long Beard: Warren Wasson, Nevada's Pioneer Indian Agent, U.S. Marshal, Inventor, and Enigma*. Minden, NV: Hot Springs Mountain Press, 2008.

Etulain, Richard W. *Lincoln and Oregon Country Politics in the Civil War Era*. Corvallis: Oregon State University Press, 2013.

———, ed. *Lincoln Looks West: From the Mississippi to the Pacific*. Carbondale: Southern Illinois University Press, 2010.

Faragher, John Mack. *Daniel Boone: The Life and Legend of an American Pioneer*. New York: Henry Holt, 1992.

Fehrenbacher, Don E. *Prelude to Greatness: Lincoln in the 1850s*. Stanford, CA: Stanford University Press, 1962.

Ferguson, Gillum. *Illinois in the War of 1812*. Urbana: University of Illinois Press, 2012.

Ficken, Robert E. *Washington Territory*. Pullman: Washington State University Press, 2002.

Fischer, David Hackett. *Albion's Seed: Four British Folkways in America*. New York: Oxford University Press, 1989.

Fitzpatrick, John, ed. *The Autobiography of Martin Van Buren*. Washington, DC: Government Printing Office, 1920 (vol. 2 of the 1918 Annual Report of the American Historical Association).

Foner, Eric. *The Fiery Trial: Abraham Lincoln and American Slavery*. New York: W. W. Norton, 2010.

———. *Free Soil, Free Labor, Free Men: The Ideology of the Republican Party before the Civil War*. New York: Oxford University Press, 1970.

———, ed. *Our Lincoln: New Perspectives on Lincoln and His World*. New York: W. W. Norton, 2008.

———. *Reconstruction: America's Unfinished Revolution, 1863–1877*. New York: Harper & Row, 1988.

———. *Who Owns History? Rethinking the Past in a Changing World*. New York: Hill & Wang, 2002.

Franklin, Benjamin. *The Autobiography of Benjamin Franklin*. Boston: Houghton Mifflin, 1896.

Franks, Kenny Arthur. *Stand Watie and the Agony of the Cherokee Nation*. Memphis: Memphis State University Press, 1979.

Frederickson, George M. *Big Enough to Be Inconsistent: Abraham Lincoln Confronts Slavery and Race*. Cambridge, MA: Harvard University Press, 2008.

Freehling, William W. *Becoming Lincoln*. Charlottesville: University of Virginia Press, 2018.

Fritz, Henry E. *The Movement for Indian Assimilation, 1860–1890*. Philadelphia: University of Pennsylvania Press, 1963.

Fry, Joseph A. *Dixie Looks Abroad: The South and U.S. Foreign Relations, 1789–1973*. Baton Rouge: Louisiana State University Press, 2002.

———. *Lincoln, Seward, and U.S. Foreign Relations in the Civil War Era.* Lexington: University Press of Kentucky, 2019.

Gentin-Pilawa, C. Joseph. *Crooked Paths to Allotment: The Fight over Federal Indian Policy after the Civil War.* Chapel Hill: University of North Carolina Press, 2012.

Gienapp, William E., and Erica L. Gienapp, eds. *The Civil War Diary of Gideon Welles, Lincoln's Secretary of the Navy.* Urbana: University of Illinois Press, 2014.

Gilpin, Alec R. *The War of 1812 in the Old Northwest.* East Lansing: Michigan State University Press, 1958.

Goodwin, Doris Kearns. *Team of Rivals: The Political Genius of Abraham Lincoln.* New York: Simon &Schuster, 2005.

Gray, Ralph D., ed. *Indiana History: A Book of Readings.* Bloomington: Indiana University Press, 1994.

Green, Michael S. *Nevada: A History of the Silver State.* Reno: University of Nevada Press, 2015.

Guelzo, Allen C. *Lincoln and Douglas: The Debates That Defined America.* New York: Simon & Schuster, 2008.

Hagan, William. *The Sac and Fox Indians.* Norman: University of Oklahoma Press, 1958.

Hall, John W. *Uncommon Defense: Indian Allies in the Black Hawk War.* Cambridge, MA: Harvard University Press, 2009.

Harris, William C. *Lincoln's Last Months.* Cambridge, MA: Harvard University Press, 2004.

Harrison, Lowell H. *Lincoln of Kentucky.* Lexington: University Press of Kentucky, 2000.

Hauptmann, Lawrence. *Between Two Fires: American Indians in the Civil War.* New York: Free Press, 1995.

Hendrick, Burton J. *Lincoln's War Cabinet.* Boston: Little, Brown, 1946.

Herndon, William H., and Jesse W. Weik. *Life of Lincoln.* Edited by Paul M. Angle. Cleveland: World Publishing, 1930.

Hirshson, Stanley P. *The White Tecumseh: A Biography of General William T. Sherman.* New York: Wiley, 1998.

Hitchcock, Caroline Hanks. *Nancy Hanks: The Story of Abraham Lincoln's Mother.* New York: Doubleday & McClure, 1900.

Hixson, Walter L. *American Settler Colonialism: A History.* New York: Palgrave Macmillan, 2013.

Hoig, Stan. *The Sand Creek Massacre.* Norman: University of Oklahoma Press, 1961.

Holt, Michael F. *The Rise and Fall of the American Whig Party: Jacksonian Politics and the Onset of the Civil War.* New York: Oxford University Press, 1999.

Horrocks, Thomas A. *Lincoln's Campaign Biographies.* Carbondale: Southern Illinois University Press, 2014.

Howe, Daniel Walker. *The Political Culture of the American Whigs*. Chicago: University of Chicago Press, 1979.

———. *What Hath God Wrought: The Transformation of America, 1815–1848*. New York: Oxford University Press, 2007.

Hubbard, Charles M., ed. *Lincoln, the Law, and Presidential Leadership*. Carbondale: Southern Illinois University Press, 2015.

Hutton, Paul Andrew, and Durwood Ball, eds. *Soldiers West: Biographies from the Military Frontier*. 2nd ed. Norman: University of Oklahoma Press, 2009.

Inskeep, Steve. *Jacksonland: President Andrew Jackson, Cherokee Chief John Ross, and a Great American Land Grab*. New York: Penguin, 2015.

Iverson, Peter. *Diné: A History of the Navajos*. Albuquerque: University of New Mexico Press, 2002.

Jackson, Harvey. *Lachlan McIntosh and the Politics of Revolutionary Georgia*. Athens: University of Georgia Press, 1979.

Johannsen, Robert W. *Frontier Politics and the Sectional Conflict: The Pacific Northwest on the Eve of the Civil War*. Seattle: University of Washington Press, 1955.

Johnson, David Alan. *Founding the Far West: California, Oregon, and Nevada, 1840–1890*. Berkeley: University of California Press, 1992.

Jones, Robert Huhn. *The Civil War in the Northwest*. Norman: University of Oklahoma Press, 1960.

Jordan, Winthrop P. *White over Black: American Attitudes toward the Negro, 1550–1812*. Chapel Hill: University of North Carolina Press, 1968.

Josephy, Alvin M. Jr. *The Civil War in the American West*. New York: Alfred A. Knopf, 1991.

Jung, Patrick J. *The Black Hawk War of 1832*. Norman: University of Oklahoma Press, 2007.

Kahan, Paul. *Amiable Scoundrel: Simon Cameron, Lincoln's Scandalous Secretary of War*. Lincoln: University of Nebraska Press, 2016.

Kaplan, Fred. *Lincoln: The Biography of a Writer*. New York: HarperCollins, 2008.

Karnes, Thomas L. *William Gilpin: Western Nationalist*. Austin: University of Texas Press, 1970.

Keller, Ron J. *Lincoln and the Illinois Legislature*. Carbondale: Southern Illinois University Press, 2019.

Kelman, Ari. *A Misplaced Massacre: Struggling over the Memory of Sand Creek*. Cambridge: Harvard University Press, 2015.

Knack, Martha C. *Boundaries Between: The Southern Paiutes, 1775–1995*. Lincoln: University of Nebraska Press, 2001.

Kohl, Lawrence Frederick. *The Politics of Individualism: Parties and the American Character in the Jacksonian Era*. New York: Oxford University Press, 1989.

Lamar, Howard R. *Dakota Territory, 1861–1889: A Study of Frontier Politics.* New Haven, CT: Yale University Press, 1956.

———. *The Far Southwest, 1846–1912: A Territorial History.* Rev. ed. Albuquerque: University of New Mexico Press, 2000.

Lander, James. *Lincoln and Darwin: Shared Visions of Race, Science, and Religion.* Carbondale: Southern Illinois University Press, 2010.

Leonard, Elizabeth D. *Men of Color to Arms! Black Soldiers, Indian Wars, and the Quest for Equality.* New York: W. W. Norton, 2010.

Lincoln, Solomon Jr. *History of the Town of Hingham, Plymouth County, Massachusetts.* Hingham, MA: Caleb Gill Jr. and Farmer & Brown, 1827.

Lincoln, Waldo. *An Account of the Descendants of Samuel Lincoln of Hingham Massachusetts: 1637–1920.* Worcester, MA: Commonwealth Press, 1923.

Lindsay, Brendan C. *Murder State: California's Native American Genocide, 1846–1873.* Lincoln: University of Nebraska Press, 2012.

Long, E. B. *The Saints and the Union: Utah Territory during the Civil War.* Urbana: University of Illinois Press, 1981.

Lowe, A. T. *The Columbian Class Book: Consisting of Geographical, Historical, and Biographical Extracts . . .* 4th ed. Worcester, MA: Dorr & Howland, 1829.

Madley, Benjamin. *An American Genocide: The United States and the California Indian Catastrophe, 1846–1873.* New Haven, CT: Yale University Press, 2009.

Madsen, Brigham. *Glory Hunter: A Biography of Patrick Edward Connor.* Salt Lake City: University of Utah Press, 1990.

Masich, Andrew E. *The Civil War in Arizona: The Story of the California Volunteers.* Norman: University of Oklahoma Press, 2006.

Maxwell, John Gary. *The Civil War Years in Utah: The Kingdom of God and the Territory That Did Not Fight.* Norman: University of Oklahoma Press, 2016.

McGinnis, Ralph Y., and Calvin N. Smith, eds. *Abraham Lincoln and the Western Territories.* Chicago: Nelson-Hall, 1994.

Miller, Darlis A. *The California Column in New Mexico.* Albuquerque: University of New Mexico Press, 1982.

Miller, Edward A. Jr. *Lincoln's Abolitionist General: A Biography of David Hunter.* Columbia: University of South Carolina Press, 1997.

Miller, Richard Lawrence. *Lincoln and His World: The Early Years: Birth to Illinois Legislature.* Mechanicsburg, PA: Stackpole Books, 2006.

Miner, H. Craig, and William E. Unrau. *The End of Indian Kansas: A Study of Cultural Revolution, 1854–1871.* Lawrence: University Press of Kansas, 1978.

*Minnesota in the Indian and Civil Wars.* 2 vols. St. Paul: Pioneer Press, 1890–93.

Moehring, Eugene P. *Urbanism and Empire in the Far West, 1840–1890*. Reno: University of Nevada Press, 2004.

Monaghan, Jay. *The Civil War on the Western Border*. Boston: Little, Brown, 1955.

Morgan, Edmund S. *American Slavery, American Freedom: The Ordeal of Colonial Virginia*. New York: W. W. Norton, 1975.

Moser, Harold D., David R. Hoth, and George H. Hoemann, eds. *The Papers of Andrew Jackson*. Vol. 4. *1816–1820*. Knoxville: University of Tennessee Press, 1994.

Moulton, Gary E. *John Ross: Cherokee Chief*. Athens: University of Georgia Press, 1978.

Nelson, Megan Kate. *The Three-Cornered War: The Union, the Confederacy, and Native Peoples in the Fight for the West*. New York: Scribner, 2020.

Nichols, David A. *Lincoln and the Indians: Civil War Policy and Politics*. St. Paul: Minnesota Historical Society Press, 2012 (reprint of 1978 edition).

Nichols, Roger L. *Black Hawk and the Warrior's Path*. Arlington Heights, IL: Harlan Davidson, 1992.

Niebuhr, Gustav. *Lincoln's Bishop: A President, a Priest, and the Fate of 300 Dakota Sioux Warriors*. New York: HarperOne, 2014.

Nugent, Walter T. K. *Habits of Empire: A History of American Expansionism*. New York: Vintage Books, 2009.

Oakes, James. *Freedom National: The Destruction of Slavery in the United States, 1861–1865*. New York: W. W. Norton, 2013.

Owens, Robert M. *Mr. Jefferson's Hammer: William Henry Harrison and the Origins of American Indian Policy*. Norman: University of Oklahoma Press, 2007.

Painter, Nell Irvin. *The History of White People*. New York: W. W. Norton, 2010.

Paludan, Phillip Shaw. *"A People's Contest": The Union and the Civil War, 1861–1865*. New York: Harper & Row, 1988.

———. *The Presidency of Abraham Lincoln*. Lawrence: University Press of Kansas, 1994.

Patterson, J. D., ed. *Life of Ma-Ka-Tai-Me-She-Kia-Kiak or Black Hawk . . .* Cincinnati: Russell, Odiorne & Metcalf, 1834.

Pease, Theodore C., and James G. Randall, eds. *The Diary of Orville Hickman Browning*. 2 vols. Springfield: Illinois State Historical Society, 1925–1933.

Peck, Graham A. *Making an Antislavery Nation: Lincoln, Douglas, and the Battle over Freedom*. Baton Rouge: Louisiana State University Press, 2017.

Perrin, William Henry. *The History of Edgar County, Illinois . . .* Chicago: William Le Baron Jr., 1879.

Peterson, Merrill D. *The Great Triumvirate: Webster, Clay, and Calhoun*. New York: Oxford University Press, 1987.

Phillips, Christopher. *The Rivers Ran Backward: The Civil War and the Remaking of the American Middle Border*. New York: Oxford University Press, 2016.

Pomeroy, Earl S. *The Territories and the United States, 1861–1890: Studies in Colonial Administration*. Philadelphia: University of Pennsylvania Press, 1947.

Portnoy, Alisse. *Their Right to Speak: Women's Activism in the Indian and Slave Debates*. Cambridge, MA: Harvard University Press, 2005.

Prentice, George D. *Biography of Henry Clay*. 2nd ed. New York: John Jay Phelps, 1831.

Prucha, Francis Paul. *The Great Father: The United States Government and the American Indian*. 2 vols. Lincoln: University of Nebraska Press, 1984.

Pryor, Elizabeth Brown. *Six Encounters with Lincoln: A President Confronts Democracy and Its Demons*. New York: Penguin, 2018.

Quigley, Paul, ed. *The Civil War and the Transformation of American Citizenship*. Baton Rouge: Louisiana State University Press, 2018.

Ramsay, David. *The Life of George Washington: Commander in Chief of the Armies of the United States of America, Throughout the War which Established Their Independence, and First President of the United States*. Edited by William Grimshaw. Baltimore: Joseph Jewitt and Cushing & Sons, 1832.

Reeve, W. Paul. *Making Space on the Western Frontier: Mormons, Miners, and Southern Paiutes*. Urbana: University of Illinois Press, 2006.

Remini, Robert V. *Henry Clay: Statesman for the Union*. New York: W. W. Norton, 1991.

Remley, David. *Kit Carson: The Life of an American Border Man*. Norman: University of Oklahoma Press, 2011.

Rice, Otis K. *Frontier Kentucky*. Lexington: University Press of Kentucky, 1975.

Richards, Leonard L. *The California Gold Rush and the Coming of the Civil War*. New York: Vintage Books, 2007.

Richardson, Elmo R., and Alan W. Farley. *John Palmer Usher: Lincoln's Secretary of the Interior*. Lawrence: University Press of Kansas, 1960.

Richardson, Heather Cox. *The Greatest Nation of the Earth: Republican Economic Policies during the Civil War*. Cambridge, MA: Harvard University Press, 1997.

———. *West from Appomattox: The Reconstruction of America after the Civil War*. New Haven, CT: Yale University Press, 2008.

Ridge, Martin. *Ignatius Donnelly: The Portrait of a Politician*. Chicago: University of Chicago Press, 1962.

Rogin, Michael Paul. *Fathers and Children: Andrew Jackson and the Subjugation of the American Indian*. New York: Random House, 1975.

Roske, Ralph J. *Everyman's Eden: A History of California*. New York: Macmillan, 1968.

Rountree, Helen C. *The Powhatan Indians of Virginia: Their Traditional Culture*. Norman: University of Oklahoma Press, 1989.

Royster, Charles W. *The Destructive War: William Tecumseh Sherman, Stonewall Jackson, and the Americans*. New York: Alfred A. Knopf, 1991.

Satz, Ronald N. *American Indian Policy in the Jacksonian Era*. Lincoln: University of Nebraska Press, 1975.

Scharff, Virginia, ed. *Empire and Liberty: The Civil War and the West*. Oakland: Autry National Center for the American West and University of California Press, 2015.

Schwantes, Carlos A. *In Mountain Shadows: A History of Idaho*. Lincoln: University of Nebraska Press, 1991.

Sheehan, Bernard. *Seeds of Extinction*. Chapel Hill: University of North Carolina Press, 1973.

Silbey, Joel H. *Party over Section: The Rough and Ready Presidential Election of 1848*. Lawrence: University Press of Kansas, 2009.

Simon, Paul. *Lincoln's Preparation for Greatness: The Illinois Legislative Years*. Norman: University of Oklahoma Press, 1965.

Smith, Adam I. P. *No Party Now: Politics in the Civil War North*. New York: Oxford University Press, 2006.

———. *The Stormy Present: Conservatism and the Problem of Slavery in Northern Politics, 1846–1865*. Chapel Hill: University of North Carolina Press, 2017.

Smith, Duane A. *The Birth of Colorado: A Civil War Perspective*. Norman: University of Oklahoma Press, 1989.

Smith, John David. *Lincoln and the U.S. Colored Troops*. Carbondale: Southern Illinois University Press, 2013.

Smith, Stacey L. *Freedom's Frontier: California and the Struggle over Unfree Labor, Emancipation, and Reconstruction*. Chapel Hill: University of North Carolina Press, 2013.

Smithers, Gregory N., and Brooke N. Newman, eds., *Native Diasporas: Indigenous Identities and Settler Colonialism in the Americas*. Lincoln: University of Nebraska Press, 2014.

Stockwell, Mary. *Interrupted Odyssey: Ulysses S. Grant and the American Indians*. Carbondale: Southern Illinois University Press, 2018.

Striner, Richard. *Lincoln and Race*. Carbondale: Southern Illinois University Press, 2010.

Strozier, Charles B. *Lincoln's Quest for Union: Public and Private Meanings*. New York: Basic Books, 1982.

Summers, Mark W. *The Plundering Generation: Corruption and the Crisis of the Union, 1849–1861*. New York: Oxford University Press, 1987.

Szasz, Ferenc Morton, and Margaret Connell Szasz. *Lincoln and Religion*. Carbondale: Southern Illinois University Press, 2014.

Taylor, Alan. *American Colonies*. New York: Penguin, 2001.

Thomas, Benjamin P. *Abraham Lincoln: A Biography*. New York: Alfred A. Knopf, 1952.

———. *Lincoln's New Salem*. Rev. ed. Chicago: Americana House, 1951.

Thompson, Jerry, ed. *Civil War in the Southwest: Recollections of the Sibley Brigade*. College Station: Texas A&M University Press, 2001.

Trask, Kerry A. *Black Hawk: The Battle for the Heart of America*. New York: Henry Holt, 2007.

Trefousse, Hans L. *Carl Schurz: A Biography*. Knoxville: University of Tennessee Press, 1982.

———. *The Radical Republicans: Lincoln's Vanguard for Racial Justice*. New York: Alfred A. Knopf, 1969.

Utley, Robert M. *Frontiersmen in Blue: The U.S. Army and the Indian*. New York: Macmillan, 1967.

———. *The Indian Frontier of the American West, 1846–1890*. Albuquerque: University of New Mexico Press, 1984.

Vaughan, Alden T. *New England Frontier: Puritans and Indians, 1620–1675*. Boston: Little, Brown, 1965.

Walters, Ronald G. *American Reformers: 1815–1860*. Rev. ed. New York: Hill & Wang, 1997.

Warde, Mary Jane. *When the Wolf Came: The Civil War and Indian Territory*. Fayetteville: University of Arkansas Press, 2013.

Warren, Louis A. *Lincoln's Youth: Indiana Years, Seven to Twenty-One, 1816–1830*. Indianapolis: Indiana Historical Society, 1959.

Watson, Harry L. *Liberty and Power: The Politics of Jacksonian America*. 2nd ed. New York: Hill & Wang, 2006.

Waugh, Joan. *U. S. Grant: American Hero, American Myth*. Chapel Hill: University of North Carolina Press, 2009.

West, Elliott. *The Contested Plains: Indians, Goldseekers, and the Rush to Colorado*. Lawrence: University Press of Kansas, 1996.

White, Richard. *Railroaded: The Transcontinentals and the Making of Modern America*. New York: W. W. Norton, 2011.

Wilentz, Sean. *The Rise of American Democracy: Jefferson to Lincoln*. New York: W. W. Norton, 2010.

Williams, Frank J. *Judging Lincoln*. Carbondale: Southern Illinois University Press, 2002.

Williams, T. Harry. *Lincoln and His Generals*. New York: Vintage Books, 1952.

Wilson, Douglas L. *Honor's Voice: The Transformation of Abraham Lincoln*. New York: Alfred A. Knopf, 1998.

———. *Lincoln before Washington: New Perspectives on the Illinois Years.* Urbana: University of Illinois Press, 1997.

Wilson, Douglas L., and Rodney O. Davis, eds. *Herndon's Informants: Letters, Interviews, and Statements about Abraham Lincoln.* Urbana: University of Illinois Press, 1998.

Wilson, Major L. *Space, Time, and Freedom: The Quest for Nationality and the Irrepressible Conflict, 1815–1861.* Westport, CT: Greenwood Press, 1974.

Winkle, Kenneth J. *Abraham and Mary Lincoln.* Carbondale: Southern Illinois University Press, 2011.

———. *The Young Eagle: The Rise of Abraham Lincoln.* Dallas: Taylor Trade, 2001.

Work, David. *Lincoln's Political Generals.* Urbana: University of Illinois Press, 2009.

Zeitz, Joshua. *Lincoln's Boys: John Hay, John Nicolay, and the War for Lincoln's Image.* New York: Penguin, 2014.

## Articles

Adams, Michael C. C. "An Appraisal of the Blue Licks Battle." *Filson Club Historical Quarterly* 75, no. 2 (Summer 2001): 181–203.

Anderson, Christopher W. "Native Americans and the Origin of Abraham Lincoln's View on Race." *Journal of the Abraham Lincoln Association* 37, no. 1 (Spring 2016): 11–29.

Aron, Stephen. "The Significance of the Kentucky Frontier." *Register of the Kentucky Historical Society* 91, no. 3 (Summer 1993): 298–323.

Bray, Robert. "What Abraham Lincoln Read—an Evaluative and Annotated List." *Journal of the Abraham Lincoln Association,* 28, no. 2 (Summer 2007): 28–81.

Bullard, F. Lauriston. "The New England Ancestry of Abraham Lincoln." *New England Magazine* 39 (1909): 685–91.

Coleman, Charles H. "Lincoln's Lincoln Grandmother." *Journal of the Illinois State Historical Society* 52, no. 1 (Spring 1959): 59–90.

Davis, Charles H. "William Gaston Coffin and His Wabash & Erie Canal Connections Revisited." *Hoosier Packet,* May 2015.

Deidrich, Mark. "Chief Hole-in-the-Day and the 1862 Chippewa Disturbance: A Reappraisal." *Minnesota History Magazine* 50, no. 5 (Spring 1987): 193–203.

Dirck, Brian. "Lincoln's Kentucky Childhood and Race." *Register of the Kentucky Historical Society* 106, nos. 3–4 (Summer/Autumn 2008): 307–32.

Floyd, Elbert F. "Insights in the Personal Friendship and Patronage of Abraham Lincoln and Anson Henry Gordon, M.D.: Letters for [*sic*] Dr. Henry to His Wife, Eliza." *Journal of the Illinois State Historical Society* 98, no. 4 (Winter 2005–06): 236–38.

Grandjean, Katherine A. "New World Tempests: Environment, Scarcity, and the Coming of the Pequot War." *William and Mary Quarterly* 68, no. 1 (Spring 2011): 75–100.

Hansen, Karen V., Ken Chih-Yan Sun, and Debra Osnowitz. "Immigrants as Settler Colonists: Boundary Work between Dakota Indians and White Immigrant Settlers." *Ethnic and Racial Studies* 40, no. 11 (2017): 1919–1938.

Harmon, Alexandra. "American Indians, American Law, and Modern American Foreign Policy." *Diplomatic History* 39, no. 5 (November 2015): 943–54.

Hendricks, Rickey L. "Henry Clay and Jacksonian Indian Policy: A Political Anachronism." *Filson Club History Quarterly* 60, no. 1 (April 1986): 218–38.

Howe, Daniel Walker. "Why Abraham Lincoln Was a Whig." *Journal of the Abraham Lincoln Association* 16, no. 1 (Winter 1995): 27–38.

Joy, Natalie. "The Indian's Cause: Abolitionists and Native American Rights." *Journal of the Civil War Era* 8, no. 2 (June 2018): 215–42.

Kantrowitz, Stephen. "White Supremacy, Settler Colonialism, and the Two Citizenships of the Fourteenth Amendment." *Journal of the Civil War Era* 10, no. 1 (March 2020): 29–53.

Kelsey, Harry. "Abraham Lincoln and American Indian Policy." *Lincoln Herald* 77, no. 3 (Fall 1975): 139–48.

———. "William P. Dole and Mr. Lincoln's Indian Policy." *Journal of the West* 10, no. 3 (July 1971): 484–92.

Kessell, John L. "General Sherman and the Navajo Treaty of 1868: A Basic and Expedient Misunderstanding." *Western Historical Quarterly* 12, no. 3 (July 1981): 251–72.

Lee, Robert, Tristan Ahtone, Margaret Pearce, and Kalen Goodluck. "Land-Grab Universities: Expropriated Indigenous Land Is the Foundation of the Land Grant University System." *High Country News* 52, no. 4 (April 2020): 32–45.

Levine, Richard R. "Indian Fights and Indian Reformers: Grant's Indian Peace Policy and the Conservative Consensus." *Civil War History* 31, no. 4 (December 1985): 329–52.

Madley, Benjamin. "Understanding Genocide in California under United States Rule, 1846–1873." *Western Historical Quarterly* 47, no. 4 (Winter 2016): 449–61.

———. "'Unholy Traffic in Human Blood and Souls': Systems of California Indian Servitude under U.S. Rule." *Pacific Historical Review* 83, no. 4 (November 2014): 626–67.

Mieder, Wolfgang. "'The Only Good Indian Is a Dead Indian': History and Meaning of a Proverbial Stereotype." *Journal of American Folklore* 106, no. 419 (Winter 1993): 38–60.

Pratt, Harry E. "Lincoln in the Black Hawk War." *Bulletin of the Abraham Lincoln Association* 54 (December 1938): 3–13.

Robinson, H. E. "The Lincoln, Hanks, and Boone Families." *Missouri Historical Review* 1, no. 1 (October 1906): 72–84.

Shoemaker, Nancy. "How Indians Got to Be Red." *American Historical Review* 102, no. 3 (June 1997): 625–44.

Silbey, Joel H. "'Always a Whig in Politics': The Partisan Life of Abraham Lincoln." *Journal of the Abraham Lincoln Association* 8, no. 1 (1996): 21–42.

Tedeger, Vincent G. "Lincoln and Territorial Patronage: The Ascendancy of the Radicals in the West." *Mississippi Valley Historical Review* 35, no. 2 (June 1948): 77–90.

Vaughan, Alden T. "From White Man to Redskin: Changing Anglo-American Perceptions of the American Indian." *American Historical Review* 87, no. 4 (October 1982): 917–53.

Vorenberg, Michael. "Abraham Lincoln and the Politics of Black Colonization." *Journal of the Abraham Lincoln Association* 14, no. 2 (Summer 1993): 22–45.

Waite, Kevin. "Jefferson Davis and Proslavery Visions of Empire in the Far West." *Journal of the Civil War Era* 6, no. 4 (December 2016): 536–65.

Warren, Louis A. "The Lincolns of Berks County." *Historical Review of Berks County* 14 (April 1949): 83–85.

———. "The Romance of Thomas Lincoln and Nancy Hanks." *Indiana Magazine of History* 30, no. 3 (September 1934): 213–22.

Watlington, Patricia. "Discontent in Frontier Kentucky." *Register of the Kentucky Historical Society* 65, no. 2 (April 1967): 77–93.

West, Elliott. "Reconstructing Race." *Western Historical Quarterly* 34, no. 1 (Spring 2003): 6–26.

Wolfe, Patrick. "Settler Colonialism and the Elimination of the Native." *Journal of Genocide Research* 8, no. 4 (2006): 387–409.

### Dissertation

Acree, Jill O. "The Sorrows of Parson Weems: His Life and Legacy." PhD diss., Claremont Graduate University, 2007.

### Government Documents

*Congressional Globe*. 31st Congress. Washington, DC: Government Printing Office, 1847–49.

*Congressional Globe*. 37th Congress. Washington, DC: Government Printing Office, 1861–63.

*Congressional Globe*. 38th Congress. Washington, DC: Government Printing Office, 1863–65.

Doolittle, James R. *Condition of the Indian Tribes: Report of the Special Committee Appointed under Joint Resolution of March 3, 1865, with Appendix [Reports of the Committees of the Senate]*. Washington, DC: Government Printing Office, 1867.

Office of Indian Affairs. *Annual Report of the Commissioner of Indian Affairs, for the Year 1861.* Washington, DC: Government Printing Office, 1861.

———. *Annual Report of the Commissioner of Indian Affairs, for the Year 1862.* Washington, DC: Government Printing Office, 1862.

———. *Annual Report of the Commissioner of Indian Affairs, for the Year 1863.* Washington, DC: Government Printing Office, 1863.

———. *Annual Report of the Commissioner of Indian Affairs, for the Year 1864.* Washington, DC: Government Printing Office, 1864.

———. *Annual Report of the Commissioner of Indian Affairs, for the Year 1865.* Washington, DC: Government Printing Office, 1865.

*Official Records of the War of the Rebellion.* Washington, DC: Government Printing Office, 1880–1901.

*Report of the Special Joint Committee on the Condition of the Indian Tribes.* 39th Congress, 2nd Session, Washington, DC: Government Printing Office, 1867.

United States Congress, House of Representatives. *Massacre of the Cheyenne Indians.* Report on the Conduct of the War, 38th Congress, 2nd Session. Washington, DC: Government Printing Office, 1865.

## Newspapers

*Christian Recorder*
*Douglass' Monthly*
*New Hampshire Sentinel* (Keene)
*New York Herald*
*New York Times*
*New York Tribune*
*San Francisco Daily Evening Bulletin*

## Internet

Abraham Lincoln Papers, Library of Congress, https://www.loc.gov/collections/abraham-lincoln-papers/.

American Presidency Project, https://www.presidency.ucsb.edu.

Lang, William L. "John Beeson (1803–1889), *The Oregon Encyclopedia,* https://web.archive.org/web/20180521020517/https://oregonencyclopedia.org/articles/beeson_john_1803_1889_/.

# INDEX

Italicized page numbers indicate figures.

**Michael S. Green**, an associate professor of history at the University of Nevada, Las Vegas, is the author or editor of three books on the Civil War, among which are *Lincoln and the Election of 1860* and *Politics and America in Crisis: The Coming of the Civil War*, and several books on Nevada, as well as dozens of articles and essays. He is on the editorial advisory board of the University of Nevada Press and is the executive director of the Pacific Coast Branch of the American Historical Association.

CONCISE
LINCOLN
LIBRARY

This series of concise books fills a need for short studies of the life, times, and legacy of President Abraham Lincoln. Each book gives readers the opportunity to quickly achieve basic knowledge of a Lincoln-related topic. These books bring fresh perspectives to well-known topics, investigate previously overlooked subjects, and explore in greater depth topics that have not yet received book-length treatment. For a complete list of current and forthcoming titles, see www.conciselincolnlibrary.com.

### *Other Books in the Concise Lincoln Library*

*Abraham Lincoln and Horace Greeley*
Gregory A. Borchard

*Lincoln and the Civil War*
Michael Burlingame

*Lincoln's Sense of Humor*
Richard Carwardine

*Lincoln and the Constitution*
Brian R. Dirck

*Lincoln in Indiana*
Brian R. Dirck

*Lincoln and the Election of 1860*
Michael S. Green

*Lincoln and Congress*
William C. Harris

*Lincoln and the Union Governors*
William C. Harris

*Lincoln and the Abolitionists*
Stanley Harrold

*Lincoln's Campaign Biographies*
Thomas A. Horrocks

*Lincoln in the Illinois Legislature*
Ron J. Keller